Table of Contents

Introduction iv

Chapter 1: The Basics of Attachment 1

Chapter 2: The Roots of Avoidant Attachment 20

Chapter 3: Daily Life With Avoidant Attachment 41

Chapter 4: Acknowledge, Reflect, Commit 62

Chapter 5: Build Emotional Intelligence and Trust 85

Chapter 6: Cultivating Self-Esteem and Resilience 107

Chapter 7: Form and Maintain Secure Relationships 127

Chapter 8: Overcome Obstacles and Embrace Change 141

Conclusion 156

References 159

Introduction

Have you ever wondered what Elsa from *Frozen*, Joey from *Friends*, and Lorelai from *Gilmore Girls* have in common? Me neither, but let me tell you anyway. These beloved characters might appear to be very different from one another. One is a literal ice queen, filled with power and a bit of a social introvert—talking to you, Elsa—while the other is a charming, player-like persona who can chat up anyone—Hi, Joey, how *you* doing? When we watch them on the screen, they don't appear to have much in common. In fact, in many ways, they seem a little opposite. But when we take a closer look, there is one important aspect they all have in common—and no, it's not their dashing good looks. It's actually their attachment style.

That's right, all three of these beloved characters can be classified as avoidant attachment-style persons. Now, I know you might wonder, "What does it matter? They're fictional!" And I know that's the case, but it matters because their fictional behavior mirrors our own reality in many ways. You know, the reality that behind our personalities, we are left with fear, uncertainty, and a deep-seated urge to protect ourselves from reign supreme. Their stories can be used to help us see our own behavior, especially when it comes to our relationships. Joey could never really move past a one-night stand, except when he fell in love with the one woman who was really off-limits and not available—Rachel. Elsa struggled to allow her sister into her life and was constantly running away from her sister's love and support—poor Anna. And, of course, Lorelai, always pushing away the guys who care about her, keeping Jason a secret from her parents so that she can keep him at arm's length, quite literally running away from Max, and convincing herself that Luke isn't the one because he won't marry her with five seconds' notice.

Avoidant Attachment Recovery Solutions:
Discover the Steps to Trust Others, Overcome Past Failures, Build Strong Relationships and Cultivate a Resilient and Positive Mindset

Dr Antonio Angleró

© **Copyright 2025 - All rights reserved.**

The content contained within this book may not be reproduced, duplicated or transmitted without direct written permission from the author or the publisher.

Under no circumstances will any blame or legal responsibility be held against the publisher, or author, for any damages, reparation, or monetary loss due to the information contained within this book, either directly or indirectly.

Legal Notice:

This book is copyright protected. It is only for personal use. You cannot amend, distribute, sell, use, quote or paraphrase any part, or the content within this book, without the consent of the author or publisher.

Disclaimer Notice:

Please note the information contained within this document is for educational and entertainment purposes only. All effort has been executed to present accurate, up to date, reliable, complete information. No warranties of any kind are declared or implied. Readers acknowledge that the author is not engaged in the rendering of legal, financial, medical or professional advice. The content within this book has been derived from various sources. Please consult a licensed professional before attempting any techniques outlined in this book.

By reading this document, the reader agrees that under no circumstances is the author responsible for any losses, direct or indirect, that are incurred as a result of the use of the information contained within this document, including, but not limited to, errors, omissions, or inaccuracies.

Copyright Case ID: 1-13882614981

Paperback: 9798332775246

Hardcover: 9798334692381

That is the crazy, heartbreaking world of the avoidant attachment style. Do you perhaps recognize some of these behaviors in your own life? So scared of commitment that you make sure it never happens, even if it means cutting your own nose to spite your face? Rather get hurt at your own hand than by someone else, right? Perhaps you've convinced yourself that an ice palace for one is the way to go, causing an eternal winter for everyone who dares to even come close? Well, my friend, then you're in the right place. Oh, and if you're looking at these characters thinking, "*That's not like me at all, but it described my partner spot on,*" stick around because this journey will be helpful to you, too.

So, what is this book all about? When I talk about *the journey*, what does that mean? Well, as you might have noticed by now, an avoidant attachment style makes it impossible to have healthy relationships. But luckily, there's something we can do about it! It can change, and we don't have to be all by ourselves all the time. Since only 55% of people feel secure in their relationships, it's safe to assume that many of us need to change our attachment style (Claridge & Barry, n.d.). That's what this journey is all about. Together, we will learn what the avoidant attachment style is and why it's not the most healthy attachment style and discuss ways to overcome and change our attachment style so that it can be healthier. But I'm not interested in helping you to just feel better momentarily. I want you to experience the transforming power of overcoming avoidant attachment theory, leading you to a fruitful and happy life. So, I won't be sugarcoating things. That doesn't mean I'll go all military on you, but I promise to keep things straightforward and call a spade a spade. That's why I make use of the A.R.C. theory.

The A.R.C. theory is tailored to individuals with avoidant attachment who want to overcome it. It dives deep into psychology, which means we get to fix our attachment style from the inside out and not just focus on the behavior. A.R.C. is an abbreviation that represents three different phases of this journey:

- A: Acknowledge.
- R: Reflect.
- C: Commit.

Part of this journey will include this method to help you overcome and experience freedom from avoidant attachment. Here's what you can expect for the rest of this journey:

- We'll start off by looking at the basics of attachment styles, which include the other—healthier—attachment styles. This will help each and every one of us to have a better understanding of where we are and where we can be.

- Next, we'll explore the roots of avoidant attachment, meaning we'll have to dig deep to find the reasoning behind our behavior. By getting to the root, we'll be able to manage it accordingly.

- After that, we'll look at what a daily life with avoidant attachment might look like, which will help you identify your own behaviors that are linked to your attachment style. Sometimes, we confuse our unhealthy behaviors with our personality and fail to consider that it's actually something that requires work and change.

- In Chapter 4, we'll use the A.R.C. method to overcome our avoidant attachment behavior. Now, this doesn't mean it's the end of the journey. In fact, in many ways, that's only the beginning. So, stick around and make sure you see the journey through if you want to see real change.

- Later, we'll look at cultivating self-esteem and resilience, which will help us to make a success of the journey and learn new, healthy behaviors to replace the old ones.

- After that, we'll explore how to form and maintain healthy and secure relationships. In other words, out with the old and in with the new!

- Finally, we'll end the journey by exploring how to overcome the obstacles we might face along the way and how to embrace this new change in our lives.

I know it sounds like a mouthful, but don't run away—even if you're tempted. You're here for a reason, so let's make a deal. I don't mind if you throw this book across the room and never pick it up again, but only once you've completed reading it. Is that a deal? You can believe this book won't change your life, but only after you've really given it a try, okay? Give it your all! Worst case scenario, nothing changes. Best case scenario, your life is transformed forever! So, whether you're a sheltered-don't-come-close-me Elsa or a player-of-the-year Joey, this is your moment to take the steps to find meaning within your relationships.

Get ready, my friend. Just like any good journey, there will be ups and downs, but man, the view will be worth it in the end! Welcome to *Avoidant Attachment Recovery Solutions,* or as I like to call it, *support group for a bunch of people who suck at relationships.* Don't worry, not for long! Not for long at all! You've got this!

Chapter 1:
The Basics of Attachment

A couple of years ago, I met a young man in a coffee shop who looked absolutely miserable. As I took a seat across from him, he wasn't too happy to share a table with a stranger at first. But after a little bit of small talk, I guess he realized I was harmless enough and not there to make his already bad day even worse. We started talking about life, and a couple of moments later, it came out that he was looking miserable because he just ditched a girl he was supposed to have a date with. "Why didn't you go?" I asked him. "You clearly look sad about not going, so why didn't you?"

He shrugged, staring out the window, contemplating my not-so-deep question. Eventually, he answered, "She's too good for me, you know. She might not see it now, but in a couple of dates, she'll see it, and then she'll leave. I'd rather just not go through all of that."

In some weird way, his logic made sense. It was an act of self-sabotage and not healthy at all, but it made sense. I felt for the guy, knowing he was stuck in an unhealthy avoidant attachment style without even realizing it. Have you ever felt like that? So scared of getting hurt that you rather just cut things off before they got too intense? I certainly have. For many years, I was a self-sabotaging, avoidant attachment guy. Too scared to really care because what if I lose it? But do you know what that got me? Loneliness, pain, and emotional turmoil. Exactly the things I tried to spare myself from. In other words, all those walls I put up to protect myself turned out to be the walls hurting me the most.

In order to really understand this behavior and the avoidant attachment theory, we need to take a step back and look at the basics of attachment. That's what this chapter is all about. We'll start by exploring the concept of attachment theory as a whole, then take a closer look at the different types of attachment styles, including secure, avoidant, anxious, and disorganized. After that, we'll look at the specific ways to recognize avoidant attachment in our own lives or in those around us who we care about. We'll also explore the impact that your attachment style can have on your personal life, career, and self-esteem. Finally, we'll end the chapter with a couple of exercises or challenges that will help you to really take what you've learned and put it into practice. What good does knowledge do when we don't apply it, right? So, we'll make sure we don't just learn but actually change our lives. With all that being said, are you ready to uncover the basics of attachment? Let's jump straight in and answer the question you might have had since the beginning: What is attachment theory even?

What Is Attachment Theory?

Attachment theory is "a cornerstone of developmental psychology that focuses on the profound significance of the bonds we forge with our primary caregivers during infancy and early childhood" (Pal, 2023). It posits that these early relationships leave a lasting imprint on our emotional development, sense of security, and how we approach relationships in the future (Cassidy et al., 2013).

The foundation of attachment theory lies in the pioneering work of British psychoanalyst John Bowlby (Main, 2023). Profoundly affected by his observations of children who had been separated from their parents during World War II, Bowlby came to believe that infants are born with an innate biological need to form close attachments with caregivers. This drive, he theorized, stems from an evolutionary need for protection and survival (Cherry, 2023). Bowlby proposed that the degree to which caregivers are responsive and attuned to a child's needs creates an internal blueprint. This blueprint, or *working model*, shapes our expectations of relationships, our capacity for trust, and how we manage emotions throughout our lives. Attachment theory holds significant weight because it

- **offers a framework for understanding human behavior:** It provides a lens through which we can understand how early relationships influence our emotional well-being, self-esteem, and ability to form healthy connections throughout life. This framework has vast implications, impacting our personal relationships, work dynamics, and even mental health.

- **explains lifelong impacts:** Attachment theory goes beyond simply explaining childhood behavior. It highlights how these early experiences shape our present and future. By understanding our attachment style, we gain valuable insight into our emotional needs, communication patterns, and coping mechanisms in both positive and negative situations.

- **informs intervention and support:** Attachment theory has become a valuable tool in various fields, including child development, education, and mental health. By understanding attachment styles, professionals can tailor interventions and support to address specific needs. This can be crucial in situations like fostering children, dealing with attachment disorders, or promoting healthy relationship development.

- **provides a basis for self-reflection:** Attachment theory empowers individuals to understand their own attachment style and its potential impact on their behavior and relationships. This self-awareness allows individuals to make informed choices, build healthier connections, and seek support when needed.

In essence, attachment theory offers a powerful framework for understanding the enduring impact of our early relationships on our lives. Its far-reaching implications touch upon diverse aspects of human experience, making it a valuable tool for both personal and professional endeavors. Different types of attachment styles provide you with more information on your own behavior and the way you behave within relationships of your own.

Different Types of Attachment Styles

Our earliest bonds with caregivers lay the groundwork for how we navigate the world and form relationships throughout our entire lives. Attachment theory explains how these early experiences translate into distinct patterns of connection, referred to as attachment styles. These styles profoundly influence our sense of security, expectations in relationships, and emotional responses. Understanding the different attachment styles can offer invaluable insights into why we act the way we do in our closest connections and empower us to build healthier, more fulfilling relationships. Let's take a look at the different types of attachment styles.

Secure Attachment Style

Within the framework of attachment theory, the secure attachment style emerges from consistent and sensitive caregiving during an individual's infancy and early childhood (Main, 2023). These caregivers are seen as reliable sources of comfort, readily available to meet the child's needs and provide consistent emotional support. As a result of this secure foundation, individuals with this attachment style:

- **Feel confident and secure in themselves:** They have a positive self-image and a strong sense of self-worth.

- **Trust others easily:** They are comfortable forming close and intimate relationships, believing that others will be generally reliable and supportive.
- **Maintain healthy emotional regulation:** They are better equipped to manage their emotions effectively and seek support when needed.
- **Communicate openly and honestly:** They feel comfortable expressing their thoughts and feelings openly and honestly within relationships.
- **Navigate conflict constructively:** They are able to work through disagreements in a healthy and productive manner.

Individuals with a secure attachment style are generally well-adjusted and thrive in various aspects of life, including personal relationships, professional settings, and overall well-being (*Secure Attachment Style*, 2021).

Avoidant Attachment Style

In contrast to the secure attachment style, the avoidant attachment style stems from early experiences where a child's emotional needs were not consistently met by their caregivers (Robinson et al., 2024). This could involve situations where caregivers were emotionally distant, unresponsive, or dismissive of the child's expressions of distress. As a result of this pattern, individuals with an avoidant attachment style often:

- **Value independence and self-reliance highly:** They prioritize being self-sufficient and may downplay the importance of close relationships.
- **Experience discomfort with intimacy and closeness:** They may feel uncomfortable with physical or emotional closeness, fearing potential engulfment or loss of independence.

- **Minimize emotional needs:** They may downplay their own emotional needs and avoid seeking support from others, believing they can handle things on their own.

- **Have difficulty expressing emotions openly:** They may struggle to express their emotions openly, fearing rejection or vulnerability.

- **Engage in distancing behavior:** In situations of conflict or emotional vulnerability, they may withdraw emotionally or physically from the relationship.

It's important to understand that this attachment style is not a conscious choice but rather a coping mechanism developed in early childhood. However, individuals with an avoidant attachment style can learn healthier ways to connect with others through self-awareness, communication techniques, and, in some cases, professional support (*Avoidant Attachment Style*, 2020).

Anxious Attachment Style

The anxious attachment style, sometimes referred to as anxious-preoccupied attachment, arises from early experiences marked by inconsistent or unpredictable caregiving (Jones, 2023). This could involve situations where caregivers were available at times but not always, or their responses to the child's needs were inconsistent, creating a sense of uncertainty and insecurity (Cafasso, 2019). As a result of this unpredictable environment, individuals with an anxious attachment style often:

- **Have a strong fear of abandonment:** They hold an intense fear of being rejected or left alone, leading to anxiety and insecurity in relationships.

- **Seek constant reassurance:** They frequently seek validation and reassurance of their partner's love and commitment.

- **Exhibit clingy behavior:** They may exhibit clingy behavior, becoming excessively reliant on their partner for emotional support. Moreover, they feel easily threatened by any perceived signs of distance.

- **Struggle with low self-esteem:** This style often coincides with low self-esteem, leading individuals to question their self-worth and constantly seek validation from others.

- **Experience jealousy and possessiveness:** They may be prone to jealousy and possessiveness, fearing their partner will find someone else more appealing.

It's crucial to remember that these characteristics are not inherent flaws but rather coping mechanisms developed in childhood to manage unpredictable caregiving. Through self-awareness, communication skills training, and, in some cases, therapy, individuals with an anxious attachment style can learn healthier ways to connect with others and build more secure relationships.

Disorganized Attachment Style

The disorganized attachment style, also known as fearful-avoidant attachment, stands apart from the other three styles due to its complex and contradictory nature (Light, 2023). It is often linked to experiences of traumatic stress during early childhood, such as neglect, abuse, or having a caregiver who is—themselves—fearful or unpredictable. Individuals with a disorganized attachment style experience a mixture of intense longing for closeness and a deep-seated fear of intimacy (Lahousen et al., 2019). This stems from the confusing and contradictory messages received from their caregivers. For example, a caregiver who is both the source of comfort and fear can create a confusing and disorienting environment for a child. As a result of this confusing dynamic, individuals with a disorganized attachment style may exhibit the following characteristics:

- **Inconsistent and unpredictable behavior:** They may swing between seeking intimacy and pushing others away, often appearing confused or apprehensive in close relationships.

- **Difficulty trusting others:** They may struggle to trust others due to their experiences of unreliable or harmful caregiving.

- **Negative self-image:** They may hold a negative self-image and believe they are unworthy of love or connection.

- **Difficulty managing emotions:** They may struggle to regulate their emotions effectively, leading to intense emotional responses and difficulty expressing their needs healthily.

- **Engaging in self-sabotaging behaviors:** They may engage in behaviors that sabotage their relationships, unconsciously recreating the same patterns of fear and uncertainty they experienced in childhood.

Understanding this attachment style is crucial, as it often stems from challenging experiences and can significantly impact an individual's ability to form healthy and secure relationships. In summary, understanding your attachment style can be highly beneficial since it can help you develop healthier coping mechanisms, build trust, and cultivate more secure connections with others.

Recognizing Avoidant Attachment Styles

Now that we have a better idea of the different attachment styles, it's essential that we know how to recognize avoidant attachment styles in our own lives and perhaps in our loved ones. So, let's take a closer look at the characteristics of avoidant attachment and what they might look like.

Individuals with avoidant attachment styles often experience difficulties in forming and maintaining close, intimate relationships. This stems from a core belief that closeness leads to vulnerability and potential for hurt. Here's a breakdown of their specific characteristics (Regan, 2023).

Struggling With Emotional Vulnerability

Avoidant people will most likely struggle to express their emotional vulnerability. Think back to our three character examples—Elsa, Joey, and Lorelai. None of them were ever very good at expressing their feelings, at least not on important matters. That's because they might want to totally avoid expressing their true feelings of affection or excitement, fearing being rejected or taking it personally if not reciprocated.

Thought Pattern: If I don't let myself get too close, I won't get hurt.

Difficulty Handling Conflict

People who are avoidant might struggle to handle conflict since everything within them screams to just run away. Just like Elsa, they might run for the hills when things get a little shaky, usually making a big mess all around them and hurting the people they love the most. They might withdraw from conversations or arguments, preferring to avoid confrontation rather than discussing issues openly. That doesn't mean that everyone who dislikes conflict is avoidant. It simply means that most people with an avoidant attachment style avoid conflict wherever they can. They might even make jokes about it and pretend like it's not a big deal.

Thought Pattern: Conflict means things are getting serious, which is risky, so I'd rather avoid it altogether.

Unwilling to Rely on Others

Avoidantly attached individuals will always strive to do everything for themselves and avoid relying on others for help. They are very independent and struggle to ask for help even with small things because they want to be sufficient. They often see relying on others as a weakness and therefore refuse to reach out to others even for emotional support.

Thought Pattern: It's safer to rely on myself. If I depend on someone, they might disappoint me, leave me, or judge me.

Trouble Reading Emotions

Avoidantly attached individuals might find it very difficult to read other people's emotions or be empathetic toward others. That's because they struggle to interpret the emotions of others accurately. They might see frustration as anger or concern as disappointment. This can lead to misunderstandings and them responding to your emotions inappropriately.

Thought Pattern: Emotions are confusing and unpredictable. Why bother trying to understand them?

Repressing or Hiding Negative Emotions

Chances are that you'll never see an avoidant attachment person cry. They are known to suppress or minimize their negative emotions, including sadness, anger, and disappointment. Think of Joey when his heart was broken. He put on a smile and was still a good friend to Rachel and Ross, even though his heart was broken. Instead, he accepted his *fate* as a heartbreaker and the *not-serious-relationship* guy.

Thought Pattern: Showing weakness through negative emotions makes me vulnerable and less desirable.

Feeling Repulsed by Intimacy

This one might not come as a surprise since emotional intimacy requires vulnerability, while avoidant attachment people usually dislike emotionally intimate relationships. It makes them uncomfortable, and they will often pull away as soon as a relationship gets serious, looking for small excuses as to why it will never work—we're looking at you, Lorelai.

Thought Pattern: Intimacy feels suffocating and threatening. I need to keep some space to protect myself.

Striving for Independence Above All

As I mentioned earlier, people with an avoidant attachment style want to be independent. In fact, they pride themselves on their independence and self-reliance. This means they often put their own needs and desires above those of others in a relationship with them and tend to be more self-serving. They are also more likely to move very slowly in a relationship, not making any sudden major moves forward—more likely to run away than move in with you.

Thought Pattern: Being independent prevents me from feeling trapped or controlled by anyone.

Uncomfortable Feeling Needed

They might shy away from situations where they feel needed or responsible for others, fearing being taken advantage of or manipulated.

Thought Pattern: *Being needed creates an obligation I might not be able to fulfill, making me vulnerable to disappointment and anger.*

Attraction to Unavailable People

They might subconsciously gravitate toward emotionally unavailable partners who reinforce their need for distance and avoid commitment.

Thought Pattern: *If they're not emotionally invested either, I don't have to get too close and risk getting hurt.*

It's important to remember that these are individual traits, and not everyone with an avoidant attachment will exhibit all of them or to the same degree.

However, understanding these characteristics can offer valuable insight into the challenges faced by individuals with this attachment style and pave the way for greater understanding and potential support strategies.

The Impact of Attachment Style on Personal and Relational Development

Our early attachment styles can have a lasting impact on various aspects of our lives, including our relationships, work, and self-esteem. As we continue on this journey, we'll dive into each of these areas, but for now, it's important that we get a general overview of how your attachment style can influence these areas of your life. Let's take a look, specifically focusing on the difference between the secure attachment and the various insecure attachments, including the avoidant attachment.

Relationships

- **Secure attachment:** Individuals with secure attachment styles tend to have fulfilling and healthy relationships. They feel comfortable expressing their emotions, trusting their partners, and engaging in open communication. They also feel comfortable relying on their partners for support and are able to navigate conflict constructively.

- **Insecure attachment:** Individuals with insecure attachment styles, such as anxious, avoidant, or disorganized, may experience difficulties in their relationships:

  - **Anxious attachment:** These individuals may crave intimacy but fear abandonment or rejection. They might exhibit *clingy* behavior or become overly worried about their partner's feelings, leading to anxiety and strain in the relationship.

  - **Avoidant attachment:** As discussed earlier, individuals with this style may struggle with intimacy, have difficulty expressing emotions, and shy away from conflict. This can lead to difficulty in forming and maintaining close relationships.

  - **Disorganized attachment:** This style is characterized by a mix of anxious and avoidant behavior, leading to inconsistent and often volatile relationships. Individuals with this style may have difficulty trusting others and struggle to maintain emotional stability within relationships.

Work

- **Secure attachment:** Individuals with secure attachment styles are often confident, reliable, and able to collaborate effectively with others. They are comfortable asking for help when needed and can navigate challenges without resorting to overdependence or emotional withdrawal.
- **Insecure attachment:** Individuals with insecure attachment styles may face challenges in the workplace:
    - **Anxious attachment:** They may struggle with trusting colleagues or supervisors, leading to difficulty delegating tasks or accepting feedback. They might also have difficulty asserting themselves or expressing their ideas due to fear of rejection.
    - **Avoidant attachment:** These individuals may prefer to work independently and avoid close relationships with colleagues. They may struggle to ask for help or collaborate effectively on projects.
    - **Disorganized attachment:** Individuals with this style may struggle with inconsistent performance, difficulty managing stress, and forming positive relationships with coworkers due to their unpredictable behavior and emotional instability.

Self-Esteem

- **Secure attachment:** Individuals with secure attachment styles typically have a healthy sense of self-worth and confidence. They are able to accept their strengths and weaknesses and navigate criticism without feeling overly defensive or discouraged.

- **Insecure attachment:** Individuals with insecure attachment styles may struggle with self-esteem due to:
    - **Anxious attachment:** The constant fear of rejection and abandonment can lead to feelings of inadequacy and worthlessness.
    - **Avoidant attachment:** The focus on self-sufficiency and detachment can mask underlying feelings of insecurity and a desire for connection that goes unmet.
    - **Disorganized attachment:** The inconsistent experiences and difficulty forming secure relationships can contribute to confusion, low self-esteem, and a feeling of not being worthy of love and support.

It's important to remember that attachment styles are not fixed. Through self-awareness, therapy, and positive experiences, individuals can learn healthier ways of relating and build more fulfilling and secure relationships in all aspects of their lives. By identifying your attachment style, whether secure, anxious, avoidant, or disorganized, you gain valuable self-awareness. This awareness is the first step toward positive change. You can begin to understand the underlying patterns in your thoughts, feelings, and behaviors in relationships. Once you recognize your attachment style, you can challenge the unhealthy thinking patterns and beliefs associated with it. For example, someone with anxious attachment might work on overcoming the fear of abandonment, while someone with avoidant attachment might address their discomfort with intimacy.

This chapter provided us with loads of information on the different attachment styles and why it's important to identify your current one. In the next chapter, we'll dive a little bit deeper into the avoidant attachment style, and how this pattern may manifest in your life. It's essential to understand the root if you want to change your attachment style for the better. But before we get there, it's time to end the chapter with a *For the Partner* and *Mindful Milestone* moment. Each chapter will end with these two sections; the first providing some additional insight and tips for the partner of the person with the avoidant attachment style, and the second helping the person with the avoidant style become more aware and mindful of their situation. Take your time as you work through these sections, and I'll see you in the next chapter!

For the Partner

Understanding your partner's attachment style, particularly if it leans toward avoidant, can be crucial for fostering a healthy and fulfilling relationship. However, navigating this dynamic requires both empathy and thoughtful communication. Here's a guide to approaching this sensitive topic.

Check Your Intentions

Before initiating a conversation, introspect upon your motivations. Are you seeking to *fix* your partner or label them? Approach this conversation with the genuine desire to understand and support your partner, not blame or criticize. Remember why you are in a relationship with them in the first place, and why they are special to you. Don't speak to them out of a place of anger or hurt but rather from a place of understanding and support. If your partner feels attacked, they might just pull away even more and shut down from you completely.

Have an Understanding

Gain a basic understanding of the attachment theory and the characteristics of avoidant attachment. This knowledge equips you to recognize the behavior patterns associated with this style and approach your partner with greater sensitivity. If you enter the conversation with no intention, information, or idea about what they might be experiencing, it might be harder for you to be patient and understanding. Having knowledge might also help them trust the information you're presenting them.

Own Your Behaviors and Patterns

When initiating a conversation, acknowledge your own role in the relationship. Share your feelings and needs openly, but avoid placing blame or making accusatory statements. Focus on "I" statements, like "I feel hurt when..." instead of "You always..."

Present the Information Kindly

Instead of focusing on the label "avoidant attachment," direct your conversation toward specific behaviors that impact you negatively. For example, instead of saying, "You're so avoidant," try, "I feel disconnected when you withdraw during disagreements."

Help Over Label

The ultimate goal is not to pigeonhole your partner with a label but to help them understand their own patterns and their impact on the relationship. Create a safe space for open and honest communication where both voices can be heard without judgment.

It's crucial to remember the following:

- **Change takes time and effort:** Avoid expecting immediate change from your partner. Patience and support are key.

- **Seek professional help:** If communication remains challenging, consider seeking professional guidance from a therapist specializing in attachment styles.

- **Focus on connection:** Ultimately, the goal is to cultivate a deeper connection and understanding in your relationship. By approaching this topic with empathy and open communication, you can create a space for individual growth and a more fulfilling partnership.

It's important to understand that avoidant behavior is often a coping mechanism formed in response to earlier experiences. Approaching your partner with compassion and a willingness to work together can foster a deeper understanding and pave the way for a more fulfilling relationship for both of you.

Mindful Milestone

Welcome to a self-discovery journey! Today, we delve into the world of attachment styles, exploring the impact they have on our lives. As a first step, we'll embark on a personal exploration by identifying your own attachment style and reflecting on the initial feelings or resistance that may arise. Take a moment to reflect on your past and present relationships, considering your emotional responses and behaviors. Answer these questions honestly, acknowledging any recurring themes:

- Do you feel comfortable expressing your needs and emotions openly in close relationships?

- How do you handle conflict in relationships? Do you tend to withdraw, become overly anxious, or seek solutions collaboratively?

- Do you find yourself feeling a constant need for reassurance from your partner or loved ones?

- Do you feel a strong sense of independence and prefer minimal emotional dependence on others?

- Have you experienced difficulty trusting or forming close bonds with others?

Based on your answers, explore the characteristics of the different attachment styles—secure, anxious, avoidant, and disorganized—and see which resonates most with your experiences. Now, grab your pen and journal! Take some time to write about your identified attachment style. Be honest with yourself and explore.

- What initial feelings arose as you identified your style?

- Was there any surprise or resistance? If so, why do you think that might be?

- Think about your past relationships. Do you see any evidence of your attachment style influencing your interactions?

- Are there any specific areas in your life where your attachment style might be impacting you?

Remember, there are no right or wrong answers here. This journaling exercise is about creating a space for self-reflection and understanding. This is just the beginning of your journey!

Chapter 2: The Roots of Avoidant Attachment

Have you ever looked at someone do something and thought, "I wonder what led you to do that?" It happens to me all the time. If someone tells a very specific joke or perhaps get annoyed by something that most people wouldn't, I can't help but wonder what let them there. But it's not just others that I question—I also look at myself when I do something or experience anything out of the ordinary. Let's make it as simple as possible by allowing me to tell you this story of Emily and John, an engaged couple who just moved into their first home together. Their home is lovely and they have everything they need, but Emily feels like there's still one thing missing: a puppy. John refuses. Why? Because he doesn't like dogs. But it's not that simple, right? Why doesn't he like dogs; or should we ask, why does Emily feel like a home needs a pet?

That's because their ideas of a dog is rooted in different childhood experiences. Emily grew up in a home where they always had pets. Her childhood dog was her best friend and consoled her after many bad dreams and broken hearts. For her, having a pet is part of the family. However, John grew up without a pet. He always wanted one, and one day, his parents came home with a puppy for him. He was so excited, but right after the news that he was getting a puppy, they told him that they were getting a divorce. For him, the puppy signified heartbreak and a broken home, something he didn't want for him and Emily.

As silly and simple as this example is, it proves one point quite clearly: there is always a root for our behavior and thoughts. Similarly, there is a root to anyone's avoidant attachment. You might not know it or you might have suppressed those childhood memories so deeply that you've forgotten about them, but there is most definitely a reason and a root for your avoidant attachment. That's exactly what we'll be exploring in this chapter. We'll start by looking at the different causes of avoidant attachment, followed by a section on exploring childhood experiences. By doing so, we'll be able to identify moments from our childhood that might have led to an avoidant attachment style.

We'll also explore the role of your parent's attachment styles and how they might have influenced you as a child, as well as how your current attachment style might influence your children. After that, we'll take some time to explore the role that past traumas and experiences can have on your attachment style, followed by a couple of psychological theories behind avoidance. As mentioned in Chapter 1, we'll end this chapter with a section for the partner to help understand their partner with avoidant attachment better, along with a mindful milestone for you. With all of that being said, let's jump straight in and get to the root of our avoidance attachment.

Common Causes of Avoidant Attachment

Understanding the common causes of avoidant attachment is important for several reasons. First, it helps us gain compassion for individuals who struggle with emotional connection and intimacy. Instead of seeing those with avoidant tendencies as cold or uncaring, we can recognize that their behaviors may stem from deep-seated insecurities rooted in their past experiences. Secondly, this understanding is crucial for promoting healthy relationships. By identifying potential causes of avoidant attachment, we can be more patient, understanding, and supportive in our interactions with people who may have this attachment style. Lastly, knowing the causes of avoidant attachment can help those affected seek appropriate therapy and work toward developing healthier and more fulfilling connections. It empowers one to break free from the patterns learned in childhood and build more secure relationships, improving their overall quality of life. So with that in mind, let's jump into the most common causes for developing an avoidant attachment style.

None Responsive Parents

When a child consistently expresses needs—crying, seeking comfort—and the parent fails to respond or show any emotional connection, the child learns that their reliance on others is unreliable. This repeated experience can lead them to develop an avoidant attachment style, seeking self-reliance as a coping mechanism.

Discouraged Crying

Crying is a natural way for infants to express needs and seek comfort. When caregivers consistently discourage crying, the child learns to suppress their emotions and disconnect from their need for connection. This can lead to difficulty expressing needs and forming healthy attachments later in life.

No Emotional Reaction

When a child's achievements or challenges are met with a consistent lack of emotional response—positive or negative—from their caregiver, they may feel a sense of emotional neglect. This can lead them to disconnect emotionally from others and develop an avoidant attachment style.

Being Made Fun Of

Experiencing ridicule or mockery for expressing emotions or seeking comfort can be incredibly damaging. It can lead the child to believe their feelings are unacceptable and discourage them from seeking connection due to fear of further ridicule. This can contribute to emotional withdrawal and an avoidant attachment style.

Annoyance

When a child's attempts to connect are met with annoyance from their caregiver, it can lead them to believe their presence and needs are a burden. This fosters feelings of insecurity and discouragement from seeking closeness, contributing to an avoidant attachment style.

Medical Issues and Nutritional Needs

While *medical issues and nutritional needs* can impact a child's emotional well-being, they are not typically considered direct causes of avoidant attachment. However, if these needs are not adequately addressed, they can create stress and strain on the caregiver-child bond, potentially contributing to insecure attachment styles.

Lack of Physical Touch

Lack of physical touch can be a factor in some cases, particularly in the early stages of development. However, it's important to remember that the quality of emotional connection is more crucial than the sheer amount of physical touch in forming secure attachments.

It's important to note that these are just some common causes, and not all individuals who experience these situations will develop an avoidant attachment style. That's why we need to really explore our own lives in order to understand where our attachment styles originated. Up next, let's take a closer look at exploring early life influences and what might have led to avoidant attachment style.

Exploring Early Life Influences

If there's one thing that the common causes for avoidant attachment revealed it's that attachment styles are deeply rooted in our experiences during early childhood, particularly in our interactions with our primary caregivers. This process of forming attachment styles involves several key aspects.

- **The need for security:** Humans are social creatures with an innate need for security and connection. Infants, especially, are highly dependent on their caregivers for basic needs and emotional well-being. This drives them to seek *proximity* and *comfort* from their primary caregivers, especially in times of distress.

- **The quality of caregiving:** The way caregivers respond to a child's needs and expressions of distress significantly impacts their developing attachment style. This includes, but is not limited to:

    o **Responsiveness:** Consistent and sensitive responsiveness to a child's needs—like feeding, soothing, and comfort—builds trust and a sense of security. Conversely, unpredictable or neglectful responses can lead to feelings of anxiety and insecurity.

    o **Emotional availability:** Caregivers who are emotionally available and attuned to the child's emotional state foster a sense of emotional safety and security. Conversely, caregivers who are emotionally distant or dismissive of the child's emotions may contribute to insecure attachment styles.

- o **Consistency:** Consistent behavior and routines provide predictable and safe environments for the child to explore and learn. Inconsistency can create confusion and anxiety, impacting attachment security.

- **Internal working models:** Based on their early experiences, children develop internal working models of themselves, others, and the world around them. These models guide their expectations and behaviors in relationships.

  - o Securely attached children develop a model where they see themselves as worthy of love and support, and others as reliable and responsive. This fosters healthy and trusting relationships.

  - o Insecurely attached children develop models where they see themselves as unlovable or unworthy, and others as unreliable or unresponsive. This can lead to difficulty in forming trusting and lasting connections.

The Role of Parents, Caregivers, and Social Environments

As we know by now, it's quite clear that parents, caregivers, and early social environments play a fundamental and impactful role in shaping one's approach to relationships throughout life. This impact is largely due to the early development of attachment styles, which are ingrained through significant interactions during infancy and early childhood. Let's take an even deeper dive into their roles.

Building Secure Attachment

When parents and caregivers consistently and sensitively respond to a child's needs—physical and emotional—they foster a sense of security, trust, and positive self-worth. This builds a foundation for secure attachment, characterized by:

- comfort with intimacy and closeness
- ability to seek and offer support
- healthy communication and conflict resolution skills
- positive outlook on relationships

Shaping Attachment Patterns

Inconsistent or unpredictable responses from caregivers can create insecure attachment, leading to:

- **Anxious attachment:** Characterized by a fear of rejection and a constant need for reassurance and closeness.
- **Avoidant attachment:** Characterized by a preference for independence and difficulty with intimacy and emotional vulnerability.
- **Disorganized attachment:** Characterized by inconsistent and unpredictable behavior patterns, often stemming from neglect or abuse.

Early Social Environment

Beyond parents and caregivers, the broader social environment plays a role. Siblings, extended family, early educational settings, and even interactions with peers can influence attachment styles. Positive interactions foster security, while negative experiences can contribute to insecurity.

Attachment styles formed in early childhood have a profound impact on how individuals approach and navigate relationships throughout their lives. They can influence

- the choice of partners and friends.
- communication patterns.
- conflict resolution skills.
- the ability to express and manage emotions.
- overall relationship satisfaction.

So, what does all of this mean? It means that the way parents, caregivers, and the early social environment interact with a child plays a crucial role in shaping their approach to relationships throughout life. By understanding the impact of attachment styles and fostering secure attachment from the beginning, we can empower individuals to create healthier, more fulfilling connections in all aspects of their lives.

The Effect of Parental Attachment Styles on Children

Understanding the effect of parental attachment styles on children is crucial when exploring your own attachment style for several reasons. Firstly, the way your parents related to you during your formative years is a major factor in shaping your own patterns of relating to others. Recognizing potential links between your parents' attachment style and your own can provide valuable insight into why you respond to relationships in certain ways. Secondly, this understanding fosters self-awareness and compassion. It can help you identify the origins of insecurities or challenges you may face in relationships, giving you perspective and reducing self-blame. Lastly, the awareness of the impact of parental attachment styles allows you to break the cycle. With effort and understanding, you can work toward developing healthier relationship patterns and potentially change the trajectory of future generations within your family. Let's take a closer look at how a parent with each of the four different attachment styles can affect their children.

Secure Attachment Style

Parents with secure attachment styles create a deeply positive impact on their children's emotional lives and relational well-being (*Attachment and Child Development*, 2023). Because these parents are comfortable with emotional intimacy and attuned to the needs of others, they consistently respond to their children's cries, frustrations, and bids for connection with warmth and sensitivity. This provides the child with a secure base for their own emotional exploration, creating confidence in their worthiness and a sense of trust that their needs will be met (Rees, 2007). Children of secure parents often develop secure attachment styles themselves, which lays the foundation for healthy relationships throughout their lives. They are able to navigate intimacy without fear, seek comfort and support when needed, and communicate their emotions and needs effectively. This security fosters a child's overall well-being, promotes positive self-esteem, and equips them for healthy, supportive relationships in the future (Pittman, 2020).

Ambivalent or Anxious-Preoccupied Attachment Style

Parents with an ambivalent or anxious-preoccupied attachment style tend to exhibit inconsistent and unpredictable behaviors toward their children (*How Attachment Styles Impact Relationships,* 2023). They may be highly responsive and attentive at times but emotionally unavailable or even intrusive at others. This inconsistency can lead to an anxious-preoccupied attachment style in the child (Cafasso, 2019). Children with this style often develop a deep-seated fear of abandonment and struggle to trust that their needs will be met. They may become overly reliant on others for reassurance and validation, leading to clinginess or neediness (Robinson et al., 2024). This can contribute to difficulty in setting boundaries and maintaining a sense of self in relationships. Additionally, they may struggle to regulate their own emotions effectively, often experiencing intense anxiety and emotional outbursts.

Avoidant Attachment Style

Parents with an avoidant attachment style often struggle to provide the consistent emotional responsiveness and connection infants require to develop a secure attachment. This can have a profound impact on their children's emotional development. Children with *avoidantly* attached parents may internalize the message that their needs are unimportant or burdensome, leading to a sense of emotional detachment and difficulty expressing their own feelings (Smith Haghighi, 2020). They may learn to suppress their emotions and withdraw from seeking comfort, leading to challenges with intimacy and vulnerability in relationships later in life (Movahed Abtahi & Kerns, 2017). Additionally, children may feel an underlying sense of insecurity and anxiety due to the lack of reliable emotional support, even if the parent does provide their basic physical needs. This can create a pattern of self-reliance and difficulty trusting others to be there for them emotionally (Li, 2022).

Disorganized Attachment Style

Parents with a disorganized attachment style often have the most profound and complex impact on their children. These parents likely have unresolved traumas or significant emotional struggles, which manifest in confusing and contradictory behaviors toward their children (Reisz et al., 2017). One moment they may be warm and nurturing, and the next, distant and neglectful. Sometimes, they may even become a source of fear for the child themselves (Drescher, 2024). This chaotic and unpredictable environment creates an overwhelming sense of disorientation, fear, and insecurity for the child. Children of parents with disorganized attachment often struggle with managing their own emotions, have difficulty building trusting relationships, and may exhibit erratic behaviors fueled by a deep sense of confusion and inner conflict. They may internalize the unpredictable nature of their early relationships and develop a deep fear of abandonment, yet simultaneously struggle to trust or allow themselves to be vulnerable with others.

Your Attachment Style and Parenting

Our early experiences with primary caregivers significantly influence how we form relationships and interact with others, including our own children. Here's how parenting might look with each of the following attachment styles:

- **Secure attachment:** Parents with this style are typically responsive to their children's needs, providing a sense of security and fostering healthy emotional development. They are also likely to use positive discipline and encourage communication.

- **Anxious-preoccupied attachment:** These parents might be overly worried about their children's well-being, leading to controlling or smothering behaviors. They may struggle to separate from their children and have difficulty setting boundaries.

- **Avoidant attachment:** Parents with this style might be emotionally distant or dismissive of their children's needs. They may prioritize independence and struggle to express affection.

- **Disorganized attachment:** This can lead to inconsistent and unpredictable parenting behavior, which can be confusing and stressful for children. Parents with this style might struggle to regulate their own emotions, making it difficult to respond effectively to their children's emotions.

It's important to note that this is a general overview, and individual experiences are complex and multifaceted. Additionally, parents can learn and develop new skills to improve their parenting regardless of their attachment style. Resources like therapy or parenting workshops can be helpful in this process. Remember, understanding the role of attachment styles can be valuable for both parents and individuals seeking to understand their own relationships and interactions with others.

The Role of Past Relationships and Traumas

Cumulative trauma, also known as *complex trauma*, refers to "repeated exposure to adverse experiences in childhood, especially those involving neglect, abuse, or violence. These experiences can have a profound and lasting impact on a person's physical and mental health" (*Understanding the Impact of Trauma*, 2014). One way this impact manifests is through the exacerbation of avoidant tendencies. Childhood cumulative trauma (CCT) encompasses various forms of maltreatment, including physical abuse, sexual abuse, emotional neglect, physical neglect, and witnessing violence. Repeated exposure to these experiences can disrupt a child's sense of safety, security, and trust in the world.

Furthermore, they may develop maladaptive coping mechanisms to navigate these overwhelming situations, which can later translate into avoidant tendencies as adults. It's important to understand that the impact of CCT and its connection to avoidant tendencies varies greatly from person to person. Several factors, such as individual resilience, access to support systems, and the severity and duration of the trauma, can influence the lasting effects. That's why there are many theories regarding this topic. Let's have a quick look at a couple in order to ensure a well-rounded understanding of how past relationships and traumas can influence your attachment style.

Continuity Hypothesis

The continuity hypothesis proposes a significant connection between our early emotional experiences and the attachment styles we develop in later relationships. This theory suggests that the way we interact with our primary caregivers in childhood, particularly in terms of their responsiveness and reliability, shapes our internal working models for future relationships (Diamond et al., 2021). Individuals with avoidant attachment styles, characterized by a fear of intimacy and a preference for emotional distance, likely had early experiences that discouraged closeness.

These experiences could have involved caregivers who were emotionally unavailable, dismissive of their needs, or inconsistent in their affection. This inconsistency or lack of reliable support can lead children to develop a perception of closeness as unreliable or even threatening. As a result, they may carry this internal working model into adulthood, subconsciously replicating the dynamics they experienced in childhood by avoiding intimacy and emotional vulnerability in their adult relationships (Diamond et al., 2021). This highlights the lasting impact of early experiences on shaping our attachment styles and emphasizes the importance of fostering secure and nurturing relationships in childhood for healthy emotional development.

Repetition Compulsion—Freudian Theory

Freudian theory offers the concept of repetition compulsion to explain how past relationships and trauma can influence attachment styles (Rafferty, 2019). This theory suggests that individuals are unconsciously driven to repeat patterns of behavior and relationships, even if these patterns are painful or unproductive. In the context of avoidant attachment, repetition compulsion can manifest as individuals repeatedly seeking out or attracting partners who reinforce their need for emotional distance. This could involve partners who are emotionally unavailable, dismissive of their needs, or prone to creating situations that trigger their fear of intimacy.

This unconscious repetition stems from a desire to master or gain control over unresolved past experiences (Esposito, 2016). By reenacting these experiences, individuals might unconsciously hope to rewrite the narrative or achieve a different outcome. However, by choosing partners who mirror their early caregivers' unavailability, they inadvertently perpetuate the very dynamic that contributed to their attachment style in the first place. This concept highlights the complex and often unconscious ways in which past experiences can influence our present choices and relationships (Cherry, 2023a). It underscores the importance of understanding and addressing underlying emotional patterns to break free from unhealthy cycles and cultivate secure and fulfilling connections.

Social Learning

Social learning theory, pioneered by Albert Bandura, sheds light on how observational learning and imitation can shape attachment styles (Main, 2022). This theory suggests that individuals, particularly in their formative years, learn social behaviors by observing and mimicking the actions and interactions of significant others, such as parents or caregivers. In the context of avoidant attachment, children who observe their primary caregivers exhibiting emotional distance, dismissiveness, or inconsistent affection may learn to adopt these behaviors themselves. This could involve replicating the caregiver's avoidance of intimacy, difficulty expressing emotions, or tendency to create emotional distance in relationships.

Through this process of observation and imitation, children develop internal models of how relationships function. They may come to believe that closeness is inherently risky or undesirable, leading them to develop an avoidant attachment style characterized by a preference for emotional distance and a fear of intimacy. Social learning theory emphasizes the importance of positive role models and nurturing environments during childhood (Main, 2022). By observing and interacting with adults who maintain healthy and secure relationships, individuals can learn valuable social and emotional skills that contribute to the development of secure attachment styles later in life.

When we look at these theories, it's clear that there's so much more to avoidant attachment than what we could possibly know already.

However, part of the journey is peeling back the layers and delving into our own lives a bit more to understand ourselves. Let's take it a step further by delving into the psyche of someone with avoidance attachment.

Understanding the Psyche of Avoidance

There's a lot that goes on in the mind without us being aware of it. It's the same when it comes to avoidance attachment. So much can get triggered by one thing that we are completely unaware of, which is why we should try to understand our thought traps, fears, and behaviors in greater detail. Here are a couple of ways through which avoidance might manifest in your psyche.

Thought Traps

- **Overgeneralization:** Taking one negative experience and applying it to all future situations. For example, "I got hurt trying to get close to someone once, so anyone I get close to will just hurt me again."

- **Mind reading:** Assuming you know what others are thinking, and believing they will reject you. For example, "They seem withdrawn; they must not be interested in being friends."

- **Catastrophizing:** Blowing up small issues into major problems and assuming the worst possible outcome. For example, "If I show them my true feelings, they'll leave me."

- **Emotional reasoning:** Believing that your emotions are facts and they reflect reality. For example, "I feel anxious and uncomfortable, so this relationship must be doomed to fail."

Fears

- **Fear of abandonment:** A deep-seated fear of being left alone or rejected, often stemming from experiences of emotional neglect or inconsistent caregiving in childhood.

- **Fear of intimacy:** A fear of getting too close to others and being vulnerable, often linked to a belief that closeness leads to pain or disappointment.

- **Fear of engulfment:** A fear of losing your sense of self or independence in a relationship, often associated with a need for control and maintaining boundaries.

Behaviors

- **Emotional withdrawal:** Distancing themselves emotionally from others to avoid feeling vulnerable or dependent. This can manifest as being physically present but emotionally unavailable.

- **Self-sufficiency:** Maintaining a strong sense of independence and relying heavily on themselves to meet their needs, often pushing away help or support from others.

- **Passive-aggressive communication:** Indirectly expressing their needs or dissatisfaction, often resorting to sarcasm, stubbornness, or giving silent treatment.

- **Difficulty expressing emotions:** Struggling to openly express their feelings, both positive and negative, often due to a fear of rejection or vulnerability.

- **Engaging in self-sabotaging behaviors:** Unconsciously creating situations that confirm their negative beliefs about relationships, ultimately leading to the very outcome they fear (e.g., pushing someone away before they get hurt).

It's important to remember that these are general patterns, and experiences can vary greatly for individuals with avoidant attachment styles. Additionally, these individuals are not inherently cold or uncaring. Their behaviors are often driven by a deep-seated fear of getting hurt and a protective mechanism they developed in response to their early experiences. Understanding your thought processes and underlying fears can foster empathy and encourage you to seek help in developing healthier attachment patterns.

For the Partner

Supporting your partner as they delve into the roots of their avoidant attachment style requires fostering a safe space built on validation and nonjudgmental communication. Here are some key strategies to create this supportive environment:

- **Active listening:** Give your partner your undivided attention, both physically and emotionally. Make eye contact, put away distractions, and avoid interrupting. Reflect back on what you hear using phrases like, "It sounds like you felt..." or, "I understand that this experience was difficult for you." This demonstrates that you're truly trying to understand their perspective without judgment.
- **Express empathy:** Acknowledge and validate their feelings, even if you don't personally understand them. Instead of minimizing their experiences with comments like, "It wasn't that bad," try phrases like, "I can see how this would be hurtful–

upsetting for you." Focus on understanding their emotional landscape rather than trying to fix or change their feelings.

- **Offer support:** Reassure your partner that you're there for them and willing to be a source of support throughout their journey. Encourage them to seek professional help from a therapist if they feel overwhelmed or need additional guidance. Respect their need for space if they need time to process their experiences and emotions on their own, but also make it clear that you're available when they're ready to talk.

By creating a safe and supportive environment, free from judgment and filled with empathy and understanding, you can empower your partner to explore their attachment style and work toward developing healthier relationship patterns. This journey of self-discovery can not only benefit them but also strengthen your relationship as you build trust and connection on a deeper level.

Mindful Milestone

Understanding your attachment style can shed light on how you form and navigate relationships. This exercise invites you to reflect on your past experiences and identify potential influences on your attachment style.

Step 1: Create a Timeline

On a timeline, list significant relationships and events in your life. This could include:

- Early childhood experiences with parents, caregivers, and siblings.
- Close friendships throughout your life.

- Romantic relationships—past and present.
- Other significant events that may have impacted your sense of security and trust, such as loss, trauma, or major life transitions.

Step 2: Reflect on Patterns

As you revisit these experiences, consider the following questions for each relationship or event:

- How did this relationship–event make you feel about yourself and others? (e.g., secure, loved, valued, rejected, isolated, etc.).
- How did this relationship–event impact your sense of trust and security? (e.g., felt safe, dependable, worried about abandonment, etc.).
- How did this relationship–event influence your communication style and emotional expression? (e.g., open communication, difficulty expressing emotions, etc.).
- Were there any recurring themes or patterns in these experiences? (e.g., difficulty getting close, repeated patterns of rejection, etc.).

Step 3: Analyze and Understand

After reflecting on your individual experiences, consider any broader patterns that emerge.

- Do you see any similarities in how you navigate different relationships?

- Are there recurring themes related to trust, intimacy, or emotional expression?

Remember, this is a journey of self-discovery, and there are no right or wrong answers. Be honest with yourself and explore your experiences openly and thoughtfully. Identifying patterns in your attachment style can be a valuable step toward understanding yourself and your relationships better. If you find yourself struggling with unhealthy attachment patterns, seeking professional guidance from a therapist can be extremely beneficial. By engaging in this self-reflection and understanding your attachment style, you can gain valuable insights into your relationships and equip yourself with tools to build healthier and more fulfilling connections in the future.

This chapter was all about getting to the root of the attachment and understanding that there is always more to the story than what it seems at first. In the next chapter, we'll continue this search for understanding by looking at what the typical daily life of an avoidant attachment individual might look like.

Chapter 3: Daily Life With Avoidant Attachment

People who are subject to avoidant attachment often get labeled as the bad guy. We imagine them as the sleezy guy you warn friends against or the mom who resents her children for being too close to her, stealing her freedom. I think many of us see them as people who have no remorse for their behavior. They break hearts and act selfishly without thinking twice, right? Well, that's actually not the case. In fact, I want to share with you a quick story from the point of view of a female friend of mine. This is what she wrote:

The knock on the door startled me. My heart hammered a frantic rhythm against my ribs, each beat echoing in the sudden silence of my apartment. I wasn't expecting anyone. In fact, I rarely was. I preferred the quiet solitude of my own company, the predictable routine of my days. The knocking persisted: A relentless insistence that chipped away at the carefully constructed walls I'd built around myself. I debated ignoring it, pretending I wasn't home. But a sliver of guilt, a foreign emotion, pricked at my conscience. Maybe it was Sarah, my neighbor, finally fed up with my constant rejections of her invitations to coffee. Or maybe, just maybe, it was David.

David. The thought sent a jolt through me. We'd met a few weeks ago at a bookstore, drawn together by a shared love of obscure poetry collections. The conversation flowed easily, his humor a stark contrast to the quiet intensity I usually presented to the world. He'd asked me out, and I, in a moment of uncharacteristic boldness, had said yes. But then came the familiar wave of panic. The fear of intimacy, of getting too close, of the inevitable disappointment when things fell apart (the way they always did). I'd texted him, making up a flimsy excuse, the guilt gnawing at me even as I typed the words.

The knocking stopped. Relief washed over me, cold and unwelcome. I retreated further into my apartment, the silence now a deafening companion. Loneliness, a familiar ache, settled in my chest. I craved connection, the warmth of shared laughter and understanding. But the fear, the ever-present fear, held me back, a prisoner of my own making. As I sat there, the echo of the unanswered knock lingering in the air, I knew something had to change. I was tired of running, of pushing people away. Maybe, just maybe, it was time to face my fear, to let someone in, even if it meant risking getting hurt. It wouldn't be easy, but maybe, just maybe, it was time to rewrite my story.

As you can see, it's not as easy as they simply don't care. Chances are, if you're reading this book, you might think that you don't have this attachment style because you care too much and actually want a relationship. But both of these things can be true. That's why this chapter will focus on how avoidant attachment can affect your daily life. This will not only provide you insight but maybe even validate some of the things you've experienced in your own life, preparing you for the transformation that is ahead. We'll start by looking at some of the most common challenges of avoidant attachment, followed by the implications that it can have on self-esteem. Once again, we'll focus on how it can affect your work and social life and how avoidant attachment might interact with other attachment styles. So, buckle up, get comfortable, and recognize that avoidant attachment doesn't mean you're heartless.

Most Common Challenges

Individuals with avoidant attachment styles often face significant challenges when forming deep and lasting intimate relationships.

These hurdles can stem from deeply ingrained patterns of behavior and thinking, often rooted in early childhood experiences. Let's delve into some of the most common obstacles.

Trust Issues

- **Fear of abandonment:** A core fear for those with avoidant attachment is the potential of being abandoned or rejected. This can make them hesitant to trust others and leave them feeling guarded and suspicious in relationships.

- **Difficulty with vulnerability:** Opening up emotionally and letting others see their true selves can be incredibly difficult for avoidant individuals. They may fear being judged or hurt, hindering the development of genuine intimacy.

Self-Reliance

- **Independent streak:** Avoidant individuals often pride themselves on their self-sufficiency and independence. They may resist relying on others or seeking emotional support, pushing potential partners away.

- **Difficulty accepting help:** The need for help can be seen as a sign of weakness, leading them to reject attempts at support from partners, even when they genuinely need it.

Emotional Distance

- **Maintaining physical and emotional boundaries:** Individuals with this attachment style often maintain a safe distance in relationships, both physically and emotionally.

This can make them appear cold or detached, creating a barrier to real connection.

- **Difficulty expressing emotions:** Openly expressing their emotions, both positive and negative, can be challenging for avoidant individuals. This can lead to miscommunication, frustration, and emotional disconnection.

Unsupportive Behavior

- **Passive-aggressive communication:** Avoidant individuals may struggle with direct communication, resorting to passive-aggressive behaviors like sarcasm or withdrawal to express their needs or desires. This can create confusion and conflict in the relationship.

- **Fear of commitment:** The prospect of long-term commitment can trigger anxiety in individuals with avoidant attachment. They may subconsciously sabotage relationships or avoid situations that lead to deeper commitment.

Feeling Suppression

- **Difficulty identifying and expressing needs:** Avoidant individuals may struggle to identify their own emotional needs and have difficulty communicating them to their partners. This can lead to feelings of resentment and unmet needs within the relationship.

- **Emotional suppression:** To cope with their fear of intimacy and potential rejection, they may suppress their emotions altogether, hindering genuine emotional connection and intimacy.

It's important to understand that these challenges are not character flaws but rather learned coping mechanisms developed in response to early experiences. With self-awareness, effort, and potentially professional guidance, individuals with avoidant attachments can learn to build healthy and fulfilling relationships.

The Implications of Avoidant Attachment on Self-Esteem

Avoidant attachment can greatly influence your self-esteem. For many, it can cause a back-and-forth swing between feeling very good about yourself followed by a deep feeling of unworthiness. Let's take a closer look at how avoidant attachment can influence both high and low self-esteem.

Low Self-Esteem

Individuals with avoidant attachment styles often find themselves locked in a battle with their own self-esteem. This attachment style is characterized by a weak self-image, leaving individuals feeling inherently inadequate and unworthy of love and connection. This core belief fuels a crippling fear of intimacy, making them hypervigilant to any potential criticism or rejection. Even minor slights or perceived disapproval can be interpreted as confirmation of their worst fears, further reinforcing their negative self-perception. The inability to form close, lasting relationships only serves to exacerbate this internal struggle. When attempts at intimacy inevitably encounter challenges, individuals with avoidant attachment often internalize the blame. They engage in harsh self-criticism, attributing the relationship's failure to their own perceived flaws and shortcomings. This reinforces the belief that they are fundamentally unlovable, creating a vicious cycle that can be difficult to break.

Furthermore, those with the fearful-avoidant attachment style experience the added burden of heightened anxiety. This anxiety fuels their fear of intimacy and makes them even more sensitive to potential rejection. They may constantly worry about being abandoned or judged, leading to social isolation and further hindering their ability to build genuine connections. The constant internal conflict between the desire for connection and the fear of rejection takes a significant toll on their mental well-being and overall sense of self-worth. It's crucial to remember that avoidant attachment is not a reflection of personal flaws or a character defect. It is a learned coping mechanism developed in response to early experiences. By understanding the roots of this attachment style and its impact on self-esteem, individuals can begin to break free from this cycle of negativity and develop healthier relationships with themselves and others.

High Self-Esteem

The picture of avoidant attachment often paints a paradox when it comes to self-esteem. While individuals with this attachment style lack a desire for deep emotional connection, they can simultaneously possess high self-esteem. This seemingly contradictory facet stems from their independent and self-reliant nature. They view themselves as capable and resourceful, needing little external validation. This confidence can manifest in being the life of the party, charming others with their wit and charisma. They may readily engage with new people but often maintain superficial connections, keeping others at arm's length. This approach allows them to maintain their autonomy and avoid the perceived vulnerability of deeper intimacy.

However, it's crucial to remember that this high self-esteem can be fragile. While they project confidence outwards, they may still harbor insecurities regarding their ability to maintain close relationships. The slightest perceived rejection, even in a superficial connection, can trigger feelings of inadequacy or self-doubt. This underlying insecurity can manifest in a dismissive attitude toward others, pushing them away to avoid potential emotional vulnerability. Therefore, while individuals with dismissive-avoidant attachment may appear confident on the surface, their self-esteem can be a delicate balance. Their independent nature fosters a sense of self-worth, but their fear of intimacy and potential rejection can create a vulnerability they strive to conceal.

The Broader Impact on Work and Social Life

In the previous chapter, we briefly touched on how avoidant attachment can affect your personal and professional life, but it goes much deeper than just that. Many people might not know this, but your attachment style can quite literally change the course of your life when it comes to personal and professional matters. Let's explore how.

Professional Life

Individuals with avoidant attachment styles can face a multitude of challenges in their professional lives due to their core beliefs around emotional intimacy and dependence on others. These challenges can manifest in various ways, impacting their interactions with colleagues, effectiveness as managers, and overall well-being in the workplace.

Firstly, they experience great difficulties in building genuine connections. While avoidant individuals might initially appear enthusiastic and invested in building connections with colleagues, their discomfort with emotional vulnerability often leads to them withdrawing and engaging in dismissive behavior over time. This can make them appear aloof and disinterested, hindering the development of genuine connections and fostering a sense of isolation within the team. This can negatively impact teamwork, collaboration, and the overall work environment, as trust and open communication are essential for effective collaboration.

Secondly, avoidant attachment individuals will often revert to emotional suppression and distancing in the workplace. They prioritize emotional independence and suppress their own emotions, creating a barrier to offering or receiving emotional support within the team. They might distance themselves from situations that require emotional engagement, appearing indifferent to the feelings of others. This can manifest as difficulty providing constructive criticism or empathetic support, leading to strained relationships and missed opportunities for deeper connection and collaboration.

Thirdly, their aversion to emotional entanglement and potential conflict can make it difficult for them to navigate and resolve workplace disagreements effectively. They might default to passive-aggressive communication styles, avoiding direct confrontation and resorting to indirect methods like sarcasm or withholding information. This can exacerbate existing conflicts, create confusion and frustration among colleagues, and hinder the team's ability to address issues constructively.

Finally, they might have a harsh and strict managing style. As managers, their tendency to maintain emotional distance can create a cold and impersonal work environment. This can be particularly detrimental to employees with anxious attachment styles, who crave validation and reassurance. Avoidant managers might struggle to provide constructive feedback, offer emotional support, or foster a sense of trust and belonging within their team. This can lead to decreased employee morale, reduced productivity, and increased employee turnover.

So, long story short, while avoidant attachment individuals are not devoid of emotions, their emphasis on emotional independence and their discomfort with vulnerability can create significant challenges in the professional sphere. These challenges can hinder their ability to build genuine connections, navigate workplace emotions effectively, and contribute to a positive and supportive work environment for themselves and their colleagues.

Social Life

Individuals with avoidant attachment styles often face difficulties in their social lives due to their discomfort with emotional closeness and vulnerability. This can manifest in several ways, creating challenges in forming and maintaining meaningful friendships.

Firstly, their fear of intimacy serves as a great challenge for deeper connection. The core of the issue lies in their apprehension toward intimate connections. They might crave social interaction but find it difficult to let others in emotionally, fearing rejection or control. This can lead to them keeping relationships superficial, avoiding situations that require deeper emotional connection, and ultimately keeping people at a distance.

Secondly, they have great difficulty with emotional reciprocity. Their preference for emotional independence can make it challenging for them to engage in the give-and-take of emotional support, which is crucial in close friendships. They might struggle to express their own emotions openly, making it difficult for friends to connect with them on a deeper level. Additionally, they might find it uncomfortable to receive emotional support, creating a one-sided dynamic and leaving friends feeling unheard and unsupported.

Thirdly, this discomfort with intimacy and emotional exchange can make it difficult to form and maintain long-lasting friendships. Friendships often require a certain level of vulnerability and emotional investment, which avoidant individuals struggle with. This can lead to them having few close friends or experiencing frequent friend group changes, as others struggle to connect with them on a deeper level and feel the relationship lacks emotional reciprocity.

Overall, the challenges associated with avoidant attachment can significantly impact an individual's social life. Their discomfort with intimacy and emotional vulnerability hinders their ability to connect with others on a deeper level, leading to difficulties forming and maintaining meaningful friendships.

Interacting With Other Attachment Styles

Now that we've confirmed that there is a much larger impact on work and personal life when you struggle with avoidant attachment, it's time to peel back another layer. Do individuals with avoidant attachments just fail to get along with everyone? Or are there certain types of attachment styles that actually might work better with them? Well, let's find out by looking at which attachment style is the most compatible with avoidant attachment and which ones are doomed from the start.

Secure Attachment With Fearful-Avoidant Attachment

The dynamic between someone with a fearful-avoidant attachment and someone with a secure attachment style can be complex, offering both potential for a healthy relationship and challenges to overcome.

Potential for a Healthy Relationship

- **Secure foundation:** The secure partner's emotional stability and comfort with intimacy can provide a safe and supportive environment for the fearful-avoidant person to gradually open up and build trust. This sense of security can encourage the fearful-avoidant partner to explore emotional vulnerability in a measured way.

- **Balance and understanding:** The secure partner's ability to express needs and emotions openly while also respecting boundaries can help the fearful-avoidant partner feel validated and understood. This fosters a balanced dynamic where both partners' needs can be met.

- **Growth and learning:** The secure partner's consistent and dependable nature can model healthy relationship behaviors for the fearful-avoidant partner. Over time, the fearful-avoidant partner might learn to express emotions more openly and navigate intimacy with greater confidence.

Challenges

- **Fear of intimacy:** The fearful-avoidant partner's discomfort with closeness might still pose challenges. The secure partner's need for emotional connection could trigger the fearful-avoidant partner's withdrawal tendencies, leading to temporary periods of distance.

- **Communication needs:** Open and honest communication is crucial. The secure partner needs to be patient and understanding of the fearful-avoidant partner's pace while also expressing their own emotional needs clearly.

The chance of compatibility between a fearful-avoidant and a secure individual is considered cautiously optimistic. While challenges exist, the secure partner's stability and emotional maturity can create a safe space for the fearful-avoidant partner to heal and grow. However, this requires consistent effort, clear communication, and a willingness from both partners to understand and support each other's needs.

Anxious With Fearful-Avoidant

The dynamic between someone with a fearful-avoidant attachment and someone with an anxious attachment can be a recipe for a roller coaster ride. Here's a breakdown of the potential interactions and compatibility.

Potential for a Healthy Relationship

Self-Awareness and Growth

If both partners are aware of their attachment styles and actively work on themselves, there's a slight chance of compatibility. The anxious partner can learn to manage their anxieties and become more secure, while the fearful-avoidant partner can gradually open up to intimacy. However, this requires significant effort and commitment from both individuals.

Challenges

- **Mismatched needs:** The anxious partner craves constant reassurance and closeness, which can feel suffocating to the fearful-avoidant partner who desires independence and fears intimacy. This creates a push-pull dynamic where the anxious partner seeks more connection, triggering the fearful-avoidant partner's withdrawal, which then fuels the anxious partner's neediness further.

- **Heightened anxiety:** The fearful-avoidant partner's emotional distance and tendency to withdraw can exacerbate the anxious partner's insecurities and fear of abandonment. This can lead to increased clinginess and anxiety in the anxious partner.

- **Communication breakdown:** Difficulty expressing needs clearly and respectfully can lead to misunderstandings and resentment. The anxious partner might misinterpret the fearful-avoidant partner's need for space as a sign of rejection, while the fearful-avoidant partner might perceive the anxious partner's clinginess as a threat to their independence.

The chance of long-term compatibility between a fearful-avoidant and an anxious individual is considered low. The fundamental needs for intimacy and independence clash significantly, creating a dynamic that can be emotionally draining for both partners.

Fearful-Avoidant With Fearful-Avoidant

The dynamic between two people with fearful-avoidant attachment styles can be a complex dance of wanting connection but fearing intimacy. Here's a breakdown of the possible interactions and compatibility.

Potential for a Healthy Relationship

Self-Awareness and Open Communication

If both partners are aware of their attachment styles and committed to open communication, there's a limited chance of compatibility. They can agree on boundaries and gradually build trust by taking small steps toward emotional intimacy. However, this requires a high level of self-awareness, patience, and a willingness to challenge their own fears.

Challenges

- **Emotional distance:** Both partners might crave connection but struggle to express vulnerability or offer emotional support. This can lead to a superficial relationship lacking depth and emotional intimacy.

- **Misunderstandings and insecurity:** The fear of being controlled or rejected can create a dynamic of mixed signals and emotional unavailability. One partner's attempt at closeness might be misinterpreted as neediness, triggering withdrawal from the other. This cycle of confusion can fuel insecurity in both partners.

- **Difficulty resolving conflict:** The shared discomfort with emotional expression can make it difficult to navigate disagreements constructively. Both partners might resort to passive-aggressive communication or avoid conflict altogether, hindering the ability to address issues effectively.

The chance of long-term compatibility between two fearful-avoidant individuals is considered low. The lack of emotional expression and the fear of vulnerability can create a stagnant and emotionally unfulfilling relationship.

Fearful-Avoidant With Dismissive-Avoidant

The dynamic between someone with a fearful-avoidant attachment and someone with a dismissive-avoidant attachment can be uncertain and hold limited potential for compatibility. Here's a breakdown of the possible interactions and challenges.

Potential for a Healthy Relationship

Unrealistic Scenario

Building a healthy and fulfilling relationship based primarily on shared avoidance of intimacy is unlikely. While both might initially find comfort in the surface-level connection, the lack of emotional depth and vulnerability can leave both partners feeling unfulfilled and isolated in the long run.

Challenges

- **Mismatched needs:** While both share a desire for independence and discomfort with intimacy, their motivations differ. The fearful-avoidant partner craves connection but fears rejection, while the dismissive-avoidant partner prioritizes independence and downplays or dismisses the need for emotional closeness altogether. This creates a dynamic where neither partner fully meets the other's needs.

- **Emotional detachment:** Both partners tend to have difficulty expressing emotions and engaging in vulnerability. This lack of emotional connection can lead to a cold and distant relationship lacking warmth and support.

- **Communication barriers:** Open and honest communication is crucial for any relationship, but both styles struggle with expressing their needs and emotions clearly. This can lead to misunderstandings, resentment, and difficulty resolving conflicts constructively.

The chance of long-term compatibility between a fearful-avoidant and a dismissive-avoidant individual is considered extremely low. The fundamental mismatch in emotional needs and the lack of emotional investment create an environment unlikely to foster a healthy and fulfilling relationship.

Dismissive-Avoidant With Dismissive-Avoidant

The dynamic between two people with dismissive-avoidant attachment styles can be a complex one, offering a sense of initial comfort but ultimately lacking the emotional connection needed for a truly fulfilling relationship. Here's a breakdown of the possible interactions and compatibility.

Potential for a Healthy Relationship

Shared Values

Both partners might initially find comfort in a relationship built on independence and a lack of emotional neediness. They may appreciate not being pressured for intimacy or vulnerability.

Challenges

- **Emotional detachment:** The core challenge lies in the lack of emotional investment from both partners. This can lead to a superficial and cold relationship lacking warmth, support, and deep connection.
- **Difficulty with conflict:** Both styles struggle with expressing emotions and navigating conflict constructively. Disagreements might be avoided altogether or dealt with through passive-aggressive communication, hindering the ability to address issues effectively.

- **Limited growth:** The avoidance of intimacy and emotional vulnerability can create a stagnant dynamic. The relationship might lack the spark and growth that often comes with emotional connection and shared experiences.

The chance of long-term compatibility between two dismissive-avoidant individuals is considered very low. The lack of emotional investment from both partners creates a dynamic that struggles to foster a truly connected and fulfilling relationship.

Secure With Dismissive-Avoidant

A secure attachment style and a dismissive-avoidant attachment style can have a relationship, but it comes with both potential and challenges.

Potential for a Healthy Relationship

- **Secure partner can provide stability:** The secure partner's emotional stability and openness can create a safe space for the dismissive-avoidant to explore intimacy gradually, at their own pace.
- **Dismissive avoidant can encourage independence:** The dismissive-avoidant's emphasis on independence can be refreshing for the secure partner who isn't afraid of alone time.

Challenges

- **Need for intimacy versus need for distance:** The secure partner's natural desire for intimacy can clash with the dismissive-avoidant's need for emotional distance. This can lead to frustration and unmet needs on both sides.

- **Communication issues:** The secure partner's openness to emotions might be met with the dismissive-avoidant's tendency to shut down or dismiss concerns. This can create communication barriers.

Overall, the success of this relationship depends on open communication and a willingness to meet each other halfway.

Anxious With Dismissive-Avoidant

The chances of this combination working out are extremely low, and it has the potential to be incredibly toxic. The only way it can possibly work is if both partners work on their self-awareness as well as their communication from the start. However, here are all the reasons it might most likely not work out.

Challenges

- **Conflicting needs:** Anxious-avoidant partners crave intimacy but fear rejection, while dismissive-avoidant partners prioritize independence and shy away from closeness. This creates a push-pull dynamic where neither partner's needs are fully met.

- **Misinterpretations:** The anxious-avoidant's need for reassurance can be seen as clinginess by the dismissive-avoidant partner. Conversely, the dismissive-avoidant partner's emotional distance can trigger the anxious-avoidant partner's fear of abandonment.

- **Communication issues:** Both styles struggle with open communication about emotions. The anxious-avoidant might become passive-aggressive, while the dismissive-avoidant might shut down conversations.

Remember, building a relationship, regardless of your attachment style, is hard work. The best way to ensure success is for both parties to strive for a secure attachment style that will lead to open communication, respect, trust, and self-awareness. So, if you feel discouraged after reading this section and believe your relationship is doomed, remember that attachment styles aren't permanent. They can change. You can change, and so can your partner. As long as you are both open and actively work toward a healthier attachment style, and considering that you're reading this book right now, I would say you're off to a good start.

For the Partner

Living with a partner who has an avoidant attachment style can present unique challenges. However, navigating interactions effectively requires patience, understanding, and clear communication. Here are some strategies that can help:

- Focus on quality time, not quantity: Instead of expecting long stretches of intense connection, prioritize quality moments of genuine connection, even if they are brief. This could involve shared activities you both enjoy or simply having dedicated conversations without distractions.

- Communicate openly but respect boundaries: Express your needs and feelings honestly, but be mindful of your partner's emotional comfort zone. Don't overwhelm them with intense emotions or expectations. Allow them space to process information and respond on their own terms.

- Avoid ultimatums or emotional manipulation: Avoid ultimatums or guilt trips, as these tactics are likely to push them further away. Instead, focus on finding solutions together and expressing your needs calmly and assertively.

- Celebrate small steps: Acknowledge and celebrate even small moments of closeness or vulnerability displayed by your partner. This positive reinforcement can encourage them to feel more comfortable opening up over time.

Remember, building a secure and fulfilling relationship with anyone takes time and effort. By practicing these strategies and fostering open communication, you and your partner can create a foundation for a lasting and healthy connection.

Mindful Milestone

Take a few deep breaths, closing your eyes if you feel comfortable. Pay attention to the sights, sounds, smells, and sensations in the present moment. Now, reflect on your day. Over the past few hours or yesterday, were there any situations where you felt a pullback or distance from someone or something? Recall a particular situation where you felt this way.

- What was the situation? Who were you with? What were you doing?

- What was your initial reaction? Did you become withdrawn or silent or tried to change the subject?

- What emotions did you experience? Did you feel uncomfortable, anxious, or fearful?

- Did you avoid expressing yourself or engaging authentically? Did you shut down emotionally or physically?

Briefly note down the situation, your reactions, and the emotions you felt. You can use a journal, phone note, or any method that works for you. This is not about criticizing yourself but simply acknowledging the patterns in your behavior. Remember, everyone has different attachment styles, and avoidant tendencies are not inherently wrong. However, understanding them can help you navigate relationships and communication more effectively. Take a few more deep breaths and carry this awareness with you. As you go about your day, notice if any similar situations arise. Observe your reactions and feelings without judgment. By practicing this mindfulness moment regularly, you can gain valuable insight into your attachment style and how it might be impacting your life.

Now that we have a better understanding of what a day in life looks like for someone with avoidant attachment, we can begin to understand ourselves a little better, as well as the others around us. This sets us up perfectly for the next chapter, where we'll take our first look at the A.R.C. method.

Chapter 4:
Acknowledge, Reflect, Commit

I once heard someone say, "Change begins with awareness and is solidified with action," and that really stuck with me through the years. That's why the A.R.C. method is such a powerful method when it comes to embracing change that is lasting and transformative. In this chapter, we'll explore this structured approach, designed to help you recognize, understand, and alter avoidant attachment behavior. But the goal is not to judge you or make you feel like you've done something wrong. Instead, I want to empower you to initiate and sustain personal change so that you'll be able to cultivate a healthy and fulfilling relationship and life.

We'll start by exploring the A.R.C. method, followed by how your past and present can influence your avoidant attachment, forcing you to behave the way you're doing. By acknowledging these truths, you'll be able to move on to the next step, where you'll reflect on your personal patterns and emotions. Finally, you'll have the opportunity to commit to change as we look at step-by-step strategies you can apply to your life. So, are you ready to embrace the A.R.C. method and the much-needed change in your life? You've got this!

The A.R.C. Method

The A.R.C. method presents a distinctive, structured approach to understanding and improving avoidant attachment. This method focuses on three key steps: Acknowledge, Reflect, and Commit, acting as a roadmap for individuals seeking to overcome the challenges associated with this attachment style. Let's explore each of these steps a letter closer.

Acknowledge

The *Acknowledge* stage, the foundation of the A.R.C. method, is crucial for individuals seeking to overcome challenges associated with avoidant attachment. This initial step revolves around a conscious recognition and acceptance of your current attachment style and its influence on your life. Here's a deeper dive into acknowledging your avoidant attachment.

Recognizing the What

- **Identifying behaviors:** This involves becoming aware of your typical reactions in situations involving intimacy, vulnerability, or conflict. Do you tend to withdraw emotionally, deflect conversations, or prioritize independence over closeness? Recognizing these avoidant behaviors is the first step toward acknowledging their impact.

- **Understanding your *why*:** Reflect on the underlying emotions associated with your avoidance. Do you fear rejection, struggle with trust, or have difficulty expressing your needs? Understanding the emotional drivers of your behavior provides valuable insight into the *why* behind your attachment style.

Recognizing the From Where

Exploring the Past

Consider the origins of your attachment style. Did you experience past relationships or an early upbringing characterized by emotional neglect, inconsistency, or unpredictability? While not aiming to blame the past, understanding potential root causes can shed light on how these experiences shaped your current attachment patterns.

Accepting Without Judgment

Self-Compassion Is Key

Avoidant attachment is not a flaw but a developed coping mechanism. Acknowledge the challenges it presents, but avoid self-criticism. Embrace self-compassion and accept yourself and where you are on your journey toward growth.

Connecting the Dots

Remember, the mindfulness exercise in the previous chapters exemplifies the Acknowledge stage. It helped you identify specific instances where your avoidant attachment manifested and explore the associated reactions and emotions. This exercise serves as a springboard for deeper self-discovery and paves the way for the next stages of the A.R.C. method, Reflect and Commit. By acknowledging your avoidant attachment with awareness, understanding, and self-compassion, you embark on a transformative journey toward secure and fulfilling relationships.

Reflect

Having acknowledged the presence and impact of avoidant attachment in your life, the A.R.C. method now guides you through *Reflect*. This second step involves deep internal exploration, allowing you to understand the consequences and underlying emotions associated with your attachment style. Here's how *Reflect* helps you navigate your inner landscape.

Examining the Impact

- **Relationships:** Reflect on how your avoidant tendencies affect your interactions with others. Do you struggle with intimacy, have difficulty maintaining healthy boundaries, or experience frequent misunderstandings? By understanding the impact on your relationships, you can identify areas for growth.

- **Overall well-being:** Explore the broader influence of your attachment style on your emotional and mental well-being. Do you experience loneliness, anxiety, or difficulty trusting others? Recognizing these impacts can motivate you to seek change.

Unveiling Emotional Responses

- **Identifying triggers:** Reflect on situations or behaviors that typically trigger your avoidance tendencies. Do you withdraw when someone gets too close, become defensive when criticized, or shut down during conflict? Identifying these triggers allows you to anticipate your reactions and develop healthier coping mechanisms.

- **Understanding your emotions:** Explore the emotions underlying your avoidance. Do you fear rejection, feel anxious about vulnerability, or struggle with expressing your needs? Understanding these emotions helps you address them effectively.

Recognizing Patterns

Connecting the Dots

Look for recurring patterns in your thoughts, feelings, and behaviors. Do you engage in self-sabotaging actions, push people away unintentionally, or have difficulty expressing positive emotions? Recognizing these patterns allows you to break free from them and build new, healthier ways of relating to yourself and others.

Building on Existing Practices

As mentioned, the mindful milestones and activities throughout this process have served as stepping stones for reflection. By observing your reactions and exploring the associated emotions, you have already engaged in the essence of the *Reflect* stage. Remember, reflection is an ongoing process. As you progress through the A.R.C. method and implement changes, continue to reflect on your experiences and reevaluate the impact of your attachment style. This ongoing process of self-discovery fuels your journey toward secure and fulfilling relationships.

Commit

Having acknowledged the presence of avoidant attachment and reflected on its impact, the A.R.C. method arrives at its final crucial step: *Commit*. This stage empowers individuals to take charge of their attachment style by actively pursuing change. Commitment involves:

- **Setting SMART goals:** Establish specific, measurable, achievable, relevant, and time-bound goals for altering your thoughts, behaviors, and relationship dynamics. Instead of aiming for a vague goal like *be less avoidant*, aim for *share one genuine feeling with my partner every day*.

- **Adopting new strategies:** Learn and implement new coping mechanisms for managing emotions, communication techniques for expressing your needs effectively, and relationship skills for building healthier connections with others.

- **Practicing consistently:** Remember, changing ingrained patterns takes time and consistent effort. Regularly practice the new strategies you've learned and integrate them into your daily interactions. The more you practice, the easier it becomes to develop new, secure attachment patterns.

Commitment in Action

- **Developing healthy coping mechanisms:** Learn how to manage your emotions effectively without resorting to avoidance.

- **Practicing assertive communication:** Discover techniques for expressing your needs and feelings in a clear, respectful, and confident manner.

- **Building secure relationships:** Understand the qualities of secure relationships and explore ways to foster healthier connections with others.

It's crucial to remember that commitment is not a one-time act but a continuous process. There will be setbacks and challenges along the way. However, by acknowledging your progress, celebrating your successes, and approaching setbacks with self-compassion, you can reinforce your commitment to creating positive change in your life and relationships. Utilizing the A.R.C. method as a whole—Acknowledge, Reflect, and Commit—equips you with the tools and framework necessary to navigate your journey toward a more secure and fulfilling attachment style. Remember, change takes time and dedication, but with consistent effort and self-compassion, you can build the relationships you deserve.

The Past and Present Influence of Avoidant Attachment

Do you remember when we spoke about the influence of the past in an earlier chapter? To recap, we've concluded that our past—the way we were raised and our childhood experiences—can greatly influence our attachment style. Now, we need to make it personal, though, and begin to acknowledge our own past and present experiences that contribute to our avoidant attachment. It's the first step of the A.R.C. method, where we get to acknowledge the moments and experiences that led us to this moment in life. Now, the goal is not to find someone else to blame for your own behavior and attachment style but to acknowledge what happened in order for you to move on with your life and reflect on your own patterns and emotions because of these experiences. For this section, we'll take a look at a couple of common things–places that can influence our attachment style. One by one, we'll explore the possibility and then acknowledge the things that might have happened within each area that contributed to our avoidant attachment style. So, are you ready to embark on the A.R.C. method? Let's get right to it!

Current Relationship Dynamics

Take a moment to reflect on your current relationships—romantic or platonic. Do you often find yourself doing or facing the following?

- Emotionally distancing when things get serious?
- Prioritizing independence over spending quality time?
- Having difficulty expressing your needs or vulnerabilities?

- Are there patterns of withdrawal or distancing when conflicts arise?
- How does your partner respond to your need for space?

Consider what might have led to this behavior. Did you see this behavior from someone else? Perhaps you were treated poorly in a previous relationship and are now mirroring that behavior to avoid getting hurt. Consider your past relationships and how each of them might have led you to this moment.

Work Environment

Up next, it's time to consider your work environment. Ask yourself the following questions:

- Does your job demand extreme self-reliance?
- Is there a lack of emotional connection with colleagues?
- Does high work stress make it hard to invest emotionally elsewhere?
- Do you find yourself avoiding team projects or social interactions at work?
- How do stress and competition at work affect your emotional openness?

Again, acknowledge if this is the case and why it might be. Have you always struggled with work, or is this something new? What idea of work environment and style did your parents model when you were little? Consider and acknowledge the different things that might have contributed to your current struggles.

Social Circle and Friendships

Take a moment to consider your social circle and your friendships. Ask yourself how your friendships function by exploring the following questions:

- Do you have a preference for superficial connections?
- Do you find it difficult to be vulnerable with even close friends?
- Is your social circle limited or constantly changing?
- Do they respect your independence over emotional sharing?

Think about past friendships and moments that might have led you here. Can you remember the first friend you ever made? What was that experience like? Did a friend hurt you at some point in your life, causing you to deeply distrust those around you? You can even take a moment to consider the idea of friendship that your parents or caregivers modeled. Did they have close, healthy friendships? By acknowledging your current situation, you are setting yourself up for future success.

Media Consumption

It's time to consider your media consumption and your ability to discern between a healthy relationship and a toxic one. Think about your media consumption and ask yourself the following questions:

- Are you exposed to portrayals of hyper-independence as desirable?
- Does social media create pressure for a perfect, self-sufficient image?

- Do you find yourself comparing your relationships to unrealistic portrayals?

- Do you find these narratives influencing your expectations or behaviors in relationships?

Consider how you currently view relationships and friendships in the media and whether they are actually healthy role models to look up to. Sure, Ross and Rachel are cute when they are happy, but man they are a toxic pairing! Carefully consider what you see as healthy and what you consider normal versus what is actually healthy—open communication, mutual respect, constructive conflict resolution, and honesty.

Societal Norms

Take a moment to consider societal norms and ask yourself the following:

- Are there messages about masculinity or femininity that discourage emotional connection?

- Does your culture emphasize self-reliance over interdependence?

- Are there any gender-specific roles that you feel like you need to adhere to when it comes to relationships and showcasing emotions? For example, men aren't allowed to cry.

These questions might be hard to answer since many of us subscribe to the societal ideas of relationships without recognizing it. When guys cry we get the *ick*, and when women cry, they are being over-emotional—as always. Take a moment to really think about the societal norms around you and whether it is something you want to adopt into your own relationship. Consider how you want to be in a relationship versus what society tells you it should be like. How do you think this has influenced your relationships? Acknowledging the role society has on your idea of a healthy relationship will help you to take the next step in overcoming it.

Personal Stressors

Lastly, we need to consider our own personal stressors and how they affect us within our relationships. Consider the following as you allow these questions to stir up some thoughts and feelings within you:

- Do you cope with stress by withdrawing from others?
- Do you have difficulty trusting others to be there for you?
- Have you experienced past rejection that makes intimacy scary?
- How do you typically cope with these stressors?

By acknowledging these behaviors in dealing with stress, you might start to notice what big of a role stress can have on you and the way you treat others. Acknowledging that your stress makes you act in a certain way will help you pinpoint ways to improve your behavior, as well as guide you on the reflection journey.

By reflecting on these areas, you can start identifying how your present and past life might be reinforcing an avoidant attachment style. Remember, this is just the first step. If you'd like to explore ways to develop a more secure attachment style, consider seeking professional help or reading resources on attachment theory. Now, we can confidently continue to the second step of the A.R.C. method and begin to reflect on our personal patterns and emotions.

Reflect on Personal Patterns and Emotions

For the reflection part of the A.R.C. method, we'll begin to reflect on how our avoidant attachment manifests within our thoughts, behaviors, and relationships. We'll make use of the three-step plan to reflect on each, ensuring we're taking our time to reflect on our own lives. Why is this so important? Because without reflection, we can't commit to change since we'll have no idea what we want to change or why it's important for us personally to change. So, with that being said, let's begin by reflecting on our avoidant thoughts.

Thoughts

Overcoming an avoidant attachment style requires recognizing and challenging the thoughts that fuel it. Here's a three-step process to help you navigate these thoughts and move toward healthier connections.

Step 1: Notice Your Thoughts

Our avoidant thoughts often operate on autopilot. The first step is to become aware of them. When faced with situations that trigger intimacy or closeness, pay attention to your inner voice. What are the automatic thoughts that pop up?

Examples of avoidant thoughts that you should notice include the following:

- They'll get too close and smother me.
- I don't need anyone. I'm better off alone.
- If I get close, I'll just get hurt again.

Step 2: Trace the Origin

Once you've identified an avoidant thought, don't judge yourself. Instead, explore its roots. Think back to experiences or messages you might have received that could have contributed to this belief.

Here are a couple of questions to ask yourself in order to trace the origin of the thought:

- Did this thought pattern stem from a past experience of rejection?
- Does it echo societal messages about independence?

Step 3: Challenge and Replace

Now that you understand the thought's origin, challenge its validity. Is this a helpful or realistic perspective? Challenge your thoughts by asking questions like:

- Is it really true that closeness always leads to being smothered?
- Can I have healthy boundaries and still be emotionally connected?

Once you've challenged the thought, replace the unhelpful thoughts with more empowering ones. For example:

- It's okay to be vulnerable; it can actually strengthen my relationships.
- I deserve healthy love and connection.

Remember, this process takes time and practice. Be patient with yourself, and celebrate your progress, no matter how small.

Behaviors

An avoidant attachment style often manifests in specific behaviors. Let's explore a three-step process to identify and adjust these behaviors, fostering healthier connections.

Step 1: Self-Observe Behavior

The first step is to become aware of your avoidant tendencies. Pay attention to your actions in social and romantic situations. Here are some signs to watch for:

- **Physical distancing:** Do you create physical space by constantly being *busy* or finding reasons to leave?
- **Emotional distancing:** Do you avoid expressing your feelings or sharing personal information?
- **Passive-aggressive communication:** Do you use sarcasm or indirectness to avoid conflict or commitment?
- **Self-sabotage:** Do you find ways to push people away before they get too close?

Keep a journal or use mindfulness techniques to track these behaviors. The more aware you are, the easier it becomes to interrupt the pattern.

Step 2: Connect Behavior to Feelings

Once you've identified an avoidant behavior, dig deeper. What emotions are driving it? Common emotions might include:

- fear of intimacy
- anxiety about vulnerability
- a subconscious belief that closeness leads to rejection

Understanding the underlying emotions can help you choose a more productive response. Ask yourself why you're doing it. What feelings are you trying to avoid? For example, "I withdraw from conversations because I'm afraid of getting hurt emotionally," or, "I cancel plans at the last minute because intimacy makes me feel anxious."

Step 3: Experiment With Change

Now that you understand the behavior and its emotional trigger, it's time to experiment with healthier responses. Here are some ideas:

- Challenge yourself to stay present in conversations even if it feels uncomfortable.
- Practice open communication by expressing your needs and feelings in a healthy way.
- Gradually increase intimacy in small steps, like sharing a personal story or initiating deeper conversations.

Remember, change takes time. It's okay if you don't get it right away. The key is to keep trying and celebrate your progress, no matter how small. Every time you choose a more secure response, you're rewiring your brain for healthier connections. If you're finding it difficult, try to open up to a trusted friend about your journey. Sharing your struggles and goals can provide valuable support and accountability.

Relationship Patterns

Overcoming an avoidant attachment style involves understanding how it affects your relationships. Here's a three-step process to gain valuable insights and pave the way for healthier connections.

Step 1: Map Out Relationships

The first step is to create a mental map of your relationships. Consider both close relationships—romantic or platonic—and casual interactions. Analyze patterns in these connections:

- **Levels of intimacy:** How comfortable are you expressing your feelings and vulnerabilities in each relationship?
- **Conflict resolution:** Do you tend to withdraw or shut down during disagreements?
- **Investment:** How much time and emotional energy do you invest in different relationships?

Use a journal or create a diagram to visualize your relationships and identify any recurring patterns related to avoidance.

Step 2: Understand the Impact

Once you've mapped your relationships, consider the impact of your avoidant tendencies. How might your behavior be affecting others?

Ask yourself: Do your partners or friends feel emotionally distant from you? Do you have difficulty maintaining long-term connections?

Thinking from the perspective of others can provide valuable insight and motivate change.

Step 3: Seek Feedback and Observe

Sometimes, the blind spots are the most important to identify. Seek honest feedback from a trusted friend, therapist, or partner—if you feel comfortable.

- **Ask them:** "Do you ever feel like I withdraw when things get emotionally intense? How do you feel about our level of intimacy?"

- **Observe their reactions:** Pay attention to both verbal and nonverbal cues to understand how your behavior affects them.

This feedback, combined with self-observation, can illuminate areas for improvement and provide valuable direction. Remember, this process is about self-discovery, not self-criticism. Be compassionate with yourself as you learn and grow.

Commit to Step-By-Step Changes and Strategies

Lastly, we're at the Commit section of the A.R.C. method, the final step, during which we focus on committing to change and the new practices that will allow you to learn healthier behaviors. Making changes, big or small, can feel daunting. But by focusing on gradual steps and utilizing the three avenues of this step, you can build a solid foundation for commitment and success.

Avenue 1: Your Belief in Your Abilities

- Identify a goal: Start by defining a specific, achievable goal you want to work on. This could be anything from improving your sleep hygiene to finally starting that exercise routine.

- Break it down: Chop your goal into smaller, more manageable steps. Think of it like climbing a staircase, not a mountain. Each step is a victory.

- Focus on past achievements: Take a moment to reflect on past challenges you've overcome. Remind yourself of your resilience and ability to learn and grow.

- Positive self-talk: Replace negative self-doubt with encouraging affirmations. Instead of "I can't do this," tell yourself, "I'm learning and making progress."

Avenue 2: Your Attitude Toward Change

1. Shift your perspective: View change not as a threat but as an opportunity for growth and self-discovery.

2. Focus on the benefits: Keep the positive outcomes of your goal in mind. Visualize the improved you and the sense of accomplishment you'll feel.

3. Celebrate every win: Acknowledge and celebrate even small victories along the way. This reinforces your positive attitude and keeps you motivated.

4. Find inspiration: Seek out stories of others who have successfully made similar changes. Their experiences can show you it's possible.

Avenue 3: Your Routine

1. Identify your routines: Pinpoint your daily and weekly routines. Are there natural spots where you can incorporate your new behavior?

2. Small tweaks, big impact: Start by adding tiny changes to your existing routines. For example, if your goal is to read

more, dedicate 10 minutes before bed to reading instead of scrolling through social media.

3. Habit stacking: Pair your new behavior with an established habit. For example, after finishing your morning coffee, do some stretches or meditate for 5 minutes.

4. Prepare for obstacles: Anticipate potential roadblocks and have a plan B. For example, if you want to cook healthier meals, prep some ingredients on weekends to avoid unhealthy takeout during busy weekdays.

Remember, change might be a lifelong pursuit, but committing to change is all in your hands. It's a decision you get to make, regardless of what you're facing. By focusing on these three avenues, you can gradually build commitment and make lasting improvements in your life. Start small, celebrate progress, and embrace the power of positive self-belief. You've got this!

For the Partner

Your partner's journey to understand and improve their attachment style through the A.R.C. method can be incredibly rewarding. As a supportive partner, you play a crucial role in creating a safe and encouraging space for them to explore and grow. Here are some ways you can be a valuable ally in this process.

Practice Reflection Together

- Open communication is key: Create a safe space for your partner to openly discuss their thoughts and feelings about attachment styles. Actively listen without judgment and express genuine interest in their self-discovery.

- Couple reflection sessions: Dedicate time for shared reflection. Explore attachment styles together, and discuss how your individual styles might interact in your relationship. Resources like online quizzes or books on attachment styles can guide your exploration.

- Celebrate each other's insights: As you both gain awareness, acknowledge and celebrate your partner's breakthroughs, no matter how small.

Show Commitment Through Empathy and Action

- Validate their feelings: Recognize the challenges and emotions that come with exploring attachment styles. Let your partner know their feelings are valid and offer reassurance throughout the process.

- Support their efforts: Encourage them to participate in activities or self-help resources that support their A.R.C. journey.

- Be patient and understanding: Change takes time and effort. There will be setbacks. Be patient and offer unwavering support, even when progress feels slow.

- Lead by example: Your partner's A.R.C. journey can be a catalyst for growth in your relationship. Be open to examining your own attachment style and actively work on improving communication and emotional vulnerability within the relationship. This creates a ripple effect of positive change.

Mindful Milestone

Let's embark on a path of self-discovery! For this mindful milestone, we'll explore your attachment. This might sound complex, but by answering some introspective questions, you can gain valuable insights. If it feels repetitive from previous chapters, remember that all of these exercises build on each other to help you understand yourself better and better every single day.

Part 1: Reflecting on Your Behaviors

Imagine yourself in a close romantic relationship. Here are some scenarios to consider:

1. **Scenario 1:** Your partner becomes distant and seems withdrawn. How do you typically react?

    A. You become anxious and try to win their affection back.

    B. You give them space but feel hurt and insecure.

    C. You calmly communicate your desire to understand what's going on.

2. **Scenario 2:** You and your partner are planning a trip. How comfortable are you delegating tasks and trusting them to handle things?

    A. You struggle to let go and prefer to micromanage everything.

    B. You feel anxious and constantly need reassurance about the plans.

C. You openly discuss preferences and share responsibilities with trust.

3. **Scenario 3:** You experience a major life stressor. How do you typically seek support from your partner?

    A. You bottle up your emotions and avoid discussing the issue.

    B. You become clingy and overly dependent on your partner for emotional support.

    C. You openly communicate your feelings and seek comfort in a healthy way.

Part 2: Exploring the Origins

Our early experiences shape our attachment styles. Reflecting on your childhood might offer clues. Were your parents generally emotionally available and supportive? Did you feel secure and loved? Remember, this is not about assigning blame but understanding the roots of your current patterns.

Part 3: Embracing Small Changes for Big Impact

No matter your attachment style, there's always room for growth. Choose one small behavior you'd like to modify based on your reflections:

- **If you identified with mostly "A" answers:** Can you practice open communication and express your needs assertively instead of resorting to anxiety-driven behaviors?

- **If you identified with mostly "B" answers:** Can you work on building trust and security within your relationship, allowing yourself to be more emotionally open?

- **If you identified with mostly "C" answers:** Fantastic! Perhaps you can focus on further strengthening your communication skills and fostering even deeper intimacy.

Remember that all of this is a journey, so keep integrating these steps into your life even as we move on to the following chapters. Up next, we'll explore emotional intelligence and trust and how we need to acquire both if we want to overcome our avoidant attachment style successfully.

Chapter 5:
Build Emotional Intelligence and Trust

Elena had always been fiercely independent. Growing up, she learned to rely on herself, building a wall around her heart. Dating felt like a constant negotiation: Intimacy threatened her autonomy, and vulnerability seemed like weakness. Relationships were fleeting, leaving a trail of emotional bruises. One day, a friend suggested a book on attachment styles. Intrigued, Elena embarked on a journey of self-discovery. She recognized her patterns: the fear of closeness, the push-pull dynamic, and the constant need for control. It was a revelation.

Armed with this awareness, Elena began the A.R.C. method. She started small, practicing open communication with a close friend. It felt awkward at first, but the honest conversation brought a sense of relief and connection she hadn't experienced before. Next, she challenged her negative beliefs about intimacy. Slowly, she started seeing vulnerability as a strength, a way to build trust and true connection. This shift in perspective opened doors. Dating remained a challenge, but this time, it felt different. Elena was more honest about her needs, setting healthy boundaries while remaining open to possibilities. When she met George, the connection was immediate. He was patient and understanding, creating a safe space for her to explore her emotions.

Their relationship unfolded organically. Elena learned to express her feelings openly, appreciating the comfort and joy of shared vulnerability. George, in turn, respected her need for independence, fostering a sense of security and trust. It wasn't always smooth sailing.

There were moments of doubt and fear, echoes of old patterns. But with each hurdle, their commitment to open communication and mutual support deepened the bond. Years later, Elena looked back on her life with a sense of gratitude. The woman she once was, guarded and distant, was a distant memory. Today, she embraced life in a loving relationship built on trust, understanding, and the courage to open up. The journey of self-discovery, fueled by a willingness to be vulnerable, had transformed her life, opening the door to a love she never thought possible.

Is this the kind of transformation you'd like to experience? Well, then, you need to cultivate emotional intelligence and trust. Luckily, that's what this chapter is all about. We'll start by exploring what emotional intelligence really is, followed by strategies to enhance emotional understanding and expression. We'll also discuss the fear of vulnerability and how it contributes to a lack of trust. So, are you ready to further transform your life for the better? Let's get to it!

What Is Emotional Intelligence?

Emotional intelligence, also known as emotional quotient (EQ), is "a multifaceted skill set that allows us to navigate the complexities of emotions" (Lafair, 2024). It involves both self-awareness and social awareness. On the one hand, we need to be able to perceive, interpret, and manage our own emotions effectively. This includes understanding the source of our feelings, regulating our emotional responses, and utilizing emotions to motivate ourselves in positive ways. On the other hand, emotional intelligence involves perceiving and interpreting the emotions of others. By effectively demonstrating our own emotions and skillfully navigating social situations, we can communicate constructively, build strong relationships, and even defuse conflict (Segal et al., 2024). Ultimately, emotional intelligence empowers us to manage stress, empathize with others, and overcome challenges, leading to a more fulfilling and successful life.

Importance of Emotional Intelligence

Emotional intelligence, as we've established, is a powerful skill set that significantly impacts personal and relational well-being. Here's how:

Personal Well-Being

- **Improved self-awareness:** By understanding your own emotions, you can manage stress more effectively, make informed decisions, and navigate challenges with a clear head.

- **Enhanced self-regulation:** Emotional intelligence equips you to control your emotional responses, preventing impulsive actions and promoting emotional stability.

- **Positive self-esteem:** When you can manage your emotions effectively, you feel more confident and capable, leading to a stronger sense of self-worth.

Relational Well-Being

- **Stronger communication:** Emotional intelligence fosters clear and empathetic communication, allowing you to express your needs and understand the needs of others.

- **Deeper connections:** The ability to perceive and respond to the emotions of others builds empathy and fosters stronger, more meaningful relationships.

- **Conflict resolution:** By effectively managing your own emotions and understanding the emotions of others, you can navigate conflict constructively and find solutions that work for everyone.

Essentially, emotional intelligence equips you with the tools to navigate your own emotional landscape and connect with others in a meaningful way. This translates to a more fulfilling personal life, marked by self-awareness and emotional stability. It also fosters strong, supportive relationships, leading to a greater sense of connection and belonging.

Strategies for Enhancing Emotional Understanding and Expression

Emotional intelligence isn't a singular skill but rather a constellation of abilities working together. It encompasses self-awareness, self-regulation, self-motivation, empathy, and communication skills. The good news is that each of these components is like a muscle: You can strengthen them with effort and dedication. By practicing self-reflection, utilizing healthy coping mechanisms, and actively seeking to understand others' perspectives, you can develop your emotional intelligence. The more you work on these areas, the more adept you'll become at managing your emotions, navigating relationships, and achieving your goals. So, don't be discouraged if you don't feel like an emotional intelligence pro right away. With consistent effort and the right strategies, you can significantly improve your EQ and become a more emotionally intelligent person. Let's take a look at a few strategies to improve the various components.

Empathy

Empathy, a cornerstone of emotional intelligence, allows us to step outside our own shoes and see the world through another's eyes. It's "the ability to understand and share the feelings of others, fostering connection and building strong relationships" (Reid, 2023). But how can we become more empathetic? Here are some tips to strengthen this crucial emotional intelligence skill:

- Active listening: Truly listen to understand, not just to respond. Pay attention to both verbal and nonverbal cues like body language and tone of voice. Ask clarifying questions to ensure you grasp the full picture of their emotions and experiences.

- Practice perspective-taking: Put yourself in the other person's shoes. Consider their background, values, and experiences that might be shaping their feelings.

- Validate their emotions: Acknowledge their emotions without judgment. Phrases like, "That sounds frustrating" or, "I can see why you'd feel hurt" can go a long way.

- Respond with compassion: Offer support and understanding. Let them know you care and are there for them.

- Embrace curiosity: Be curious about others' experiences. Ask open-ended questions to learn more about their feelings and perspectives.

- Read fiction: Getting lost in a good book allows you to experience the world through another character's eyes. This can be a great way to practice empathy in a safe space.

- Volunteer or help others: Helping those in need can build empathy by exposing you to different experiences and fostering a sense of connection.

- Mindfulness practice: Mindfulness exercises like meditation can help you become more aware of your own emotions, which is a crucial first step in understanding others' emotions.

Self-Awareness

Self-awareness is all about understanding your inner world. It's "the ability to recognize your emotions, thoughts, and motivations and how they influence your behaviors." By developing strong self-awareness, you gain the power to navigate your emotions effectively and make conscious choices that align with your values. But how can you cultivate this crucial skill? Here are some tips to improve self-awareness as part of your emotional intelligence journey:

- Journaling: Take time each day, even just a few minutes, to journal your thoughts and feelings. This creates a space for self-reflection and can help you identify patterns in your emotions and reactions.

- Identify your triggers: Pay attention to situations or people who consistently trigger negative emotions in you. Understanding your triggers empowers you to manage your responses proactively.

- Practice mindfulness: Mindfulness exercises like meditation can help you become more aware of your present moment experience, including your emotions, thoughts, and bodily sensations. This heightened awareness allows you to observe your emotions without judgment.

- Seek feedback: Ask trusted friends, colleagues, or a therapist for honest feedback on how you come across different situations. This external perspective can provide valuable insights into your blind spots.

- Analyze your behavior: Reflect on your actions and reactions. Ask yourself why you behaved a certain way and what emotions might have been driving your behavior.

- Strengths and weaknesses: Identify your strengths and weaknesses. Understanding your capabilities and limitations allows you to play to your strengths and work on areas for improvement.

- Celebrate your emotions: Don't shy away from your emotions. Acknowledge and accept all your feelings, both positive and negative. By understanding your emotional landscape, you gain greater control over your responses.

- Body check-ins: Throughout the day, take a moment to pause and check in with your body. Notice any physical sensations that might be linked to your emotions. For example, a tight jaw could indicate stress, while a racing heart might signal anxiety.

Communication Skills

Communication skills are the foundation of strong relationships and a crucial aspect of emotional intelligence. They encompass both verbal and nonverbal abilities that allow us to effectively express our thoughts, feelings, and needs while also understanding the messages of others. Clear communication fosters trust, builds rapport, and helps us navigate conflict constructively. But how can we hone these essential skills? Here are some tips to improve communication skills as part of your emotional intelligence journey:

- Empathy in action: As we already mentioned, put yourself in the other person's shoes and try to understand their perspective. This allows for more compassionate and effective communication.

- Clear and concise communication: Express yourself clearly and concisely, avoiding vagueness or overly complicated language. Tailor your communication style to your audience for better understanding.

- Nonverbal communication: Nonverbal cues like body language, eye contact, and facial expressions play a significant role in communication. Be mindful of your nonverbal signals and ensure they align with your verbal message.

- "I" statements: When expressing concerns or disagreements, use "I" statements to take ownership of your feelings.

- Validate others' emotions: Acknowledge and validate the emotions of others, even if you don't agree with them. Phrases like, "It sounds like you're feeling upset" or, "I can see why you'd be frustrated" can go a long way in fostering positive communication.

- Conflict resolution: Approach disagreements with a collaborative mindset, aiming to find solutions that work for everyone involved. Practice active listening and be open to compromise.

- Effective feedback: When providing feedback, focus on specific behaviors and offer suggestions for improvement. Frame your feedback in a constructive and respectful manner.

- Open-ended questions: Use open-ended questions to encourage conversation and deeper understanding. This allows the other person to elaborate on their thoughts and feelings.

- Active body language: Maintain good eye contact, nod your head to show you're engaged, and avoid crossed arms or closed postures that can signal disinterest.

Self-Regulation

Self-regulation, a key component of emotional intelligence, refers to "your ability to manage your emotions and impulses effectively" (Landry, 2019). It's about staying calm under pressure, thinking clearly before reacting, and guiding your behavior toward your long-term goals. Strong self-regulation allows you to navigate challenging situations with grace and make choices that align with your values. But how can you develop this vital skill? Here are some tips to improve self-regulation as part of your emotional intelligence journey:

- Recognize your Triggers: The first step to managing your emotions is being aware of what triggers them. Pay attention to situations, people, or events that consistently evoke strong emotional responses. Once you identify your triggers, you can develop proactive strategies to manage your reactions.

- Practice mindfulness: Mindfulness exercises like meditation help you become more aware of your emotions in the present moment. By observing your emotions without judgment, you can choose your response rather than letting your emotions dictate your behavior.

- Develop calming techniques: Equip yourself with healthy coping mechanisms to manage difficult emotions. Deep breathing exercises, progressive muscle relaxation, and visualization are all effective techniques to calm yourself down in the heat of the moment.

- Take a time out: If you feel overwhelmed by emotions, take a time out to cool down before reacting. Excuse yourself from the situation and take a few minutes to compose yourself.

- Challenge negative thoughts: Our thoughts significantly influence our emotions. When you notice negative self-talk, challenge those thoughts and reframe them in a more positive and realistic light.

- Delay gratification: Learning to delay gratification is a crucial aspect of self-regulation. Don't give in to impulsive urges. Take a moment to consider the potential consequences before acting.

- Practice delayed reaction: Instead of reacting immediately to a situation that triggers you, take a pause. Give yourself a mental *time out* to assess the situation and formulate a thoughtful response.

- Express yourself assertively: Learn to communicate your needs and feelings assertively but respectfully. Bottling up emotions can lead to outbursts later.

- Identify your limits: Recognize your limitations and don't take on more than you can handle. Saying no to additional commitments when you're already stretched thin can help prevent stress and emotional overload.

- Focus on solutions: When faced with challenges, focus on finding solutions rather than dwelling on the problem. A problem-solving mindset empowers you to take control of the situation and manage your emotions effectively.

Self-Motivation

Self-motivation, the engine that drives emotional intelligence, is "the force that compels you to take action and achieve your goals. It's the internal fire that pushes you forward, even when faced with challenges or setbacks." Strong self-motivation allows you to initiate and persevere, transforming your aspirations into reality (Eatough, 2022). But how can you stoke the flames of your inner drive? Here are some tips to improve self-motivation as part of your emotional intelligence journey:

- Set SMART goals: Start by setting Specific, Measurable, Achievable, Relevant, and Time-bound (SMART) goals. Clear and well-defined goals give you a sense of direction and purpose, fueling your motivation.

- Visualize success: Take time to vividly imagine yourself achieving your goals. This mental rehearsal can boost your confidence and motivation to take action.

- Break down big goals: Large, overwhelming goals can feel paralyzing. Break them down into smaller, manageable steps. Completing these mini-victories provides a sense of accomplishment and keeps you motivated on your quest.

- Identify your *why*: Connect your goals to your core values and passions. Understanding the *why* behind your goals adds meaning and purpose, fueling your intrinsic motivation.

- Reward yourself: Celebrate your achievements, big and small. Rewards reinforce positive behavior and keep you motivated to continue progressing toward your goals.

- Positive self-talk: Challenge negative self-doubt with positive affirmations. Believe in yourself and your capabilities—your inner voice has a powerful influence on your motivation.

- Find inspiration: Surround yourself with positive and motivated people. Their energy and success stories can be contagious, boosting your own motivation.

- Focus on progress: Don't get discouraged by setbacks. Focus on the progress you've made and celebrate your journey. Remember, it's not about perfection but consistent effort and growth.

- Embrace challenges: View challenges as opportunities for learning and growth. Overcoming obstacles can be a powerful motivator and build your resilience.

By incorporating these tips into your life, you'll become a more emotionally intelligent communicator. You'll build stronger relationships, navigate conflict more effectively, and achieve better outcomes in all your interactions.

The Fear of Vulnerability

Vulnerability can be defined as "a state of emotional exposure that carries a degree of uncertainty" (Fritscher, 2019). It involves a willingness to be open and authentic, expressing your true feelings and desires. This openness comes with an inherent emotional risk: the possibility of getting hurt or rejected. In simpler terms, being vulnerable means being willing to take a chance on love, connection, and honest expression despite the fear of being hurt. This can be challenging, but it's a crucial aspect of building strong relationships and living a truly fulfilling life. People with avoidant attachment styles often have a deep-seated fear of vulnerability. This fear stems from their early experiences with caregivers. There are a few common fears and misconceptions about vulnerability that people with avoidant attachment believe. Let's take a closer look at busting some of these myths once and for all.

Common Fears and Misconceptions About Vulnerability

Ultimately, we want to overcome the fear of vulnerability in order to have deep and meaningful relationships. But it's easier said and done, especially when there are so many misconceptions regarding vulnerability, particularly among avoidant-attached individuals. So, let's take a look at some of these misconceptions to overcome them.

Vulnerability Is Weakness

While society often views vulnerability as a weakness, it's actually a strength that unlocks deeper connections and personal growth. Sharing your feelings and experiences requires emotional intelligence—the ability to understand and manage your own emotions while recognizing those of others. This openness fosters trust in relationships. By showing someone you trust them enough to be your authentic self, you create a stronger bond. Note that it takes courage to be vulnerable, exposing yourself to potential rejection. However, this willingness demonstrates inner strength and confidence.

Vulnerability also breeds connection. When you share your struggles, it allows others to connect with you on a deeper level. They can empathize with your experiences and offer compassion. This shared vulnerability fosters a sense of shared humanity. You may discover others have faced similar challenges, creating a sense of belonging and strengthening your relationships in all aspects of life.

Finally, vulnerability fosters growth. By being vulnerable, you engage in self-reflection, examining your emotions and experiences to gain a deeper understanding of yourself and your motivations. Processing difficult emotions through vulnerability builds resilience for future challenges. Stepping outside your comfort zone and being vulnerable allows for significant personal growth. You learn to embrace your imperfections and become more comfortable with your authentic self. Vulnerability isn't about oversharing but creating space for genuine connections and fostering personal growth: a strength to be embraced, not a weakness to be feared.

I Don't Do Vulnerability

The phrase "I don't do vulnerability" often trips up individuals with avoidant attachment styles. It stems from a deeply ingrained belief that vulnerability equates to weakness and leaves them exposed to potential hurt. While self-protection is a natural human response, completely avoiding vulnerability hinders the ability to forge secure and fulfilling connections.

Here's why the *no vulnerability* stance backfires: Vulnerability isn't about recklessly baring your soul or naively trusting everyone. It's about allowing yourself to be seen and heard authentically, with all your strengths and imperfections. For those with avoidant attachment, this feels like a terrifying tightrope walk. Early experiences of emotional neglect or rejection might have led them to build towering walls to protect themselves. However, these walls create a barrier to intimacy and emotional closeness. By shutting down vulnerability, they miss out on the rich tapestry of human connection—the empathy, compassion, and support that come from being truly seen and understood by another.

Imagine vulnerability as a bridge, not a tightrope. It allows for a cautious exploration of connection and a gradual lowering of defenses to build trust and intimacy. While there's always a risk of emotional exposure, the potential rewards—a deep sense of belonging, supportive relationships, and a more fulfilling life—far outweigh the fear. By embracing vulnerability in small, manageable ways, individuals with avoidant attachments can learn to build secure and lasting connections. It's a journey, not a destination, but one that can lead to a more enriching and emotionally fulfilling life.

Vulnerability Is Letting It All Hang Out

The misconception that vulnerability is simply letting it all hang out is a common hurdle when exploring this concept. It paints a picture of emotional oversharing or reckless disclosure, leaving you feeling exposed and potentially judged. True vulnerability is far more nuanced. It's not about blurting out every detail of your life or burdening others with your every worry.

Instead, vulnerability involves a thoughtful sharing of your authentic self and expressing your feelings and experiences in an appropriate way. It's about creating a safe space for genuine connection, where you feel comfortable enough to be open and honest without the pressure of being perfect. Vulnerability allows you to share your joys, triumphs, and, yes, even your struggles and insecurities.

Imagine vulnerability as a carefully curated conversation, not an emotional outburst. It requires discernment and choosing the right person and the right time to share your inner world. By fostering trust and emotional intimacy, vulnerability allows for deeper connections and fosters a sense of shared humanity. It's about creating space for empathy and compassion, not about seeking validation or unloading every burden. So, next time you hesitate to be vulnerable, remember it's not about reckless exposure but about creating a foundation for meaningful connections built on trust and shared experiences.

We Can Go At It Alone

Avoidant attachment individuals might cling to the belief that they can go at it alone, a misconception that can lead to isolation and missed opportunities for connection. This self-sufficiency often stems from a history of emotional unavailability in their caregivers. Having learned to rely on themselves for comfort and support, they might feel a deep sense of distrust and a fear of depending on others who might not be there for them.

However, the illusion of complete independence comes at a cost. Humans are social creatures wired for connection. While solitude can be refreshing, chronic isolation can take a toll on mental and emotional well-being. By shutting themselves off from potential relationships, avoidant individuals miss out on the joys of companionship, the support system strong bonds can provide, and the emotional intimacy that comes with vulnerability and trust.

The truth is, even the strongest among us need help sometimes. Building a network of supportive relationships doesn't diminish one's strength; it allows you to weather life's storms with a safety net and a source of encouragement. Learning to rely on others in a healthy and balanced way is a sign of strength, not weakness. It allows avoidant individuals to tap into a wellspring of support and enrich their lives with meaningful connections.

After busting these misconceptions and myths, it's clear that we need to overcome the fear of vulnerability. Let's take a look at how that can happen.

Overcoming the Fear of Vulnerability

Letting your guard down and being vulnerable can feel terrifying. Society often portrays it as a weakness, leaving you exposed and defenseless. But the truth is, vulnerability is a superpower waiting to be unleashed. It's the key to unlocking deeper connections, fostering personal growth, and living a more authentic life. Here's how you can gradually confront and embrace vulnerability as your strength:

- Permission to be you: Start by giving yourself permission to be your true self, flaws and all. Vulnerability isn't about perfection; it's about embracing your unique journey. When you accept yourself, you create space for others to accept you, too.

- Growth mindset: Vulnerability provides a springboard for learning and growth. By opening yourself to new experiences and sharing your struggles, you gain valuable insights and perspectives that can shift your mindset and help you navigate life's challenges.

- Feelings into action: Vulnerability empowers you to fully embrace your emotions—the good, the bad, and the ugly. Don't shy away from difficult feelings. Instead, acknowledge them, understand them, and use them to guide your actions in a healthy and appropriate way.

- Embrace new experiences: Stepping outside your comfort zone is a powerful way to practice vulnerability. Say yes to new experiences, even if they scare you a little. Vulnerability allows you to embrace the unknown and discover hidden strengths and possibilities.

- Quieting the critic: One of the biggest hurdles to vulnerability is the fear of judgment. Actively challenge those negative thoughts. Realize that most people are preoccupied with their own worries, and those who matter will accept you for who you are.

- Self-compassion is key: Practicing self-compassion is crucial for embracing vulnerability. Treat yourself with kindness and understanding, just as you would a loved one. Remember, everyone makes mistakes and experiences setbacks. Vulnerability allows you to learn from them and grow without harsh self-criticism.

Vulnerability isn't about becoming a doormat or letting others walk all over you. It's about allowing yourself to connect on a deeper level, build genuine relationships, and experience the richness of life. It's a journey, not a destination, and with each step, you'll discover the immense strength that lies within your vulnerability. However, vulnerability is impossible without trust, which is why we should focus on establishing trust on this expedition.

Practical Exercises for Establishing Trust

Individuals with avoidant attachment styles often struggle with building trust due to a history of emotional unavailability from caregivers. This might have instilled a deep-seated fear of intimacy and a belief that relying on others leads to disappointment. They may build walls to protect themselves, making it difficult to truly connect with others and be vulnerable. This hesitation to open up makes it challenging to establish the foundation of trust necessary for strong, lasting relationships. But since trust is something that can be built, let's take a look at a couple of practical exercises to work on establishing trust:

- Open communication: Foster open and honest communication. Talk about your feelings, needs, and expectations. Actively listen to your partner's perspective and validate their emotions.

- Respectful interactions: Treat your partner with respect, even during disagreements. Avoid personal attacks, name-calling, or yelling. Focus on the issue at hand and approach it collaboratively.

- Healthy boundaries: Establish clear and healthy boundaries for both yourself and your partner. This shows respect for each other's individual needs and creates a safe space within the relationship.

- Assume the best: When faced with an ambiguous situation, give your partner the benefit of the doubt. Communicate your concerns openly, but try to approach things with a positive intention in mind.

- Vulnerability is key: Practice vulnerability by sharing your feelings and experiences with your partner. This allows them to see you in a more authentic light and fosters a deeper connection.

For the Partner

Loving someone with an avoidant attachment style can be a beautiful yet complex journey. Their natural tendency to shy away from intimacy can make building trust a challenge. However, with patience, understanding, and the right approach, you can create a safe and trusting environment that fosters a deeper connection. Here are some tips to guide you:

- Be a safe haven: Strive to be a source of comfort and security for your partner. Avoid criticism or judgment, and create a space where they feel comfortable expressing their emotions without fear of rejection.

- Respect their boundaries: Avoidant individuals often have clear boundaries around their need for alone time and space. Respect these boundaries without taking it personally. Give them the time and space they need to recharge and feel secure.

- Focus on the positive: Acknowledge and appreciate your partner's efforts, big or small, to connect with you. Positive reinforcement encourages them to continue opening up and building trust.

- Avoid pushing for intimacy: Don't pressure your partner to disclose more than they're comfortable with. Pushing for intimacy can backfire, causing them to withdraw further. Let trust develop organically.

- Focus on shared activities: Engage in activities that you both enjoy and that don't require deep emotional vulnerability right away. Shared hobbies or interests can create a sense of connection without putting pressure on intimacy.

- Be patient: Building trust takes time and consistent effort. Avoid getting discouraged by setbacks. Celebrate small victories and acknowledge the progress, no matter how slow.

- Lead by example: Demonstrate your own vulnerability by sharing your feelings and experiences in an appropriate way. This can create a safe space for your partner to eventually feel comfortable doing the same.

Every relationship is unique. These tips can serve as a starting point, but it's important to tailor your approach to your partner's specific needs and comfort level. Consider seeking professional guidance if you need help navigating communication challenges or require additional support in building a trusting bond.

Mindful Milestone

For this mindful milestone, we'll be focusing on rebuilding trust in relationships. To get a personal understanding of the challenges and rewards involved, I invite you to participate in a trust exercise with a close friend or family member:

1. Find a safe, open space where you won't be interrupted.
2. Stand back-to-back, with each person placing their arms out to the side.
3. The person designated as the *trustor* will gently lean back, trusting the other person—the *catcher*—to catch them.
4. Once caught, switch roles and repeat the exercise.

After completing the exercise, take some time to journal about your experience. Here are some prompts to guide your reflection:

- Emotional responses: How did you feel during the exercise? Were you nervous, scared, or excited? Did your emotions differ when you were the trustor or the catcher?

- Challenges faced: Did you encounter any challenges during the exercise? Did trust come easily, or were there moments of hesitation? How did you overcome these challenges?

- Importance of communication: Did communication play a role in the exercise? How did verbal or nonverbal cues impact your sense of trust?

- Building trust takes time: Reflect on the idea that trust isn't built overnight but through consistent actions and open communication. How does this relate to your experience in the exercise?

Remember, there are no right or wrong answers here. Be honest with yourself about your experience and how it relates to trust in your relationships. Think about how the insights you gained from this exercise can be applied to your everyday interactions with friends, family, and romantic partners. How can you foster a sense of trust and build stronger, more meaningful relationships?

After completing these exercises, take a moment to process all that you've accomplished so far. Then, move on to the next chapter, where we'll talk about cultivating self-esteem and resilience.

Chapter 6:
Cultivating Self-Esteem and Resilience

Did you know that over 85% of people will, at some point, find themselves wrestling with the gremlins of self-doubt and insecurity? (Perera, 2020). This statistic, while seemingly overwhelming, offers a hidden comfort: You are far from alone in this experience. Feeling unsure of yourself is a universal human condition, not a character flaw. The good news? It doesn't have to be a permanent resident in your mind. There are many people out there who have successfully combatted self-doubt, but it doesn't just happen overnight and without additional effort. As someone with an avoidant attachment style, you aren't immune to self-doubt. In fact, a lot of the behaviors of someone with avoidant attachment have undertones of self-doubt and low levels of resilience. That's why you need to put in the work to overcome negative self-talk and embrace resilience.

This chapter is your roadmap to cultivating a robust sense of self-esteem and resilience. We'll embark on a transformative journey, exploring how to shift your perspective, nurture a positive self-image, and build the inner strength to weather life's inevitable storms. By the time we reach the final page, you'll be well on your way to forging a stronger, more confident you, ready to embrace life's challenges with newfound resilience. Let's start by exploring negative self-perception and the impact it can have on your life.

Negative Self-Perception

Negative self-perception, a harsh inner critic whispering insecurities, is a common human experience. Its roots run deep, often stemming from a complex interplay of past experiences. Childhood experiences with neglectful or critical caregivers, societal pressures to conform to unrealistic beauty standards, personal setbacks, or even seemingly minor instances of negative feedback can all leave their mark, shaping a distorted self-image. This constant internal chatter takes a significant toll on mental well-being. Imagine being bombarded with negativity day in and day out. It's no surprise, then, that negative self-perception reinforces unhelpful thought patterns, fuels feelings of inadequacy, and erodes self-esteem. Over time, this relentless self-criticism can spiral further, leading to a sense of hopelessness, helplessness, and worthlessness—hallmarks of depression.

This impact is particularly pronounced in individuals with avoidant attachment styles. Formed in early childhood through inconsistent or unavailable caregivers, avoidant attachment is characterized by a deep fear of intimacy and a strong need for independence. This fear often stems from a negative self-perception: a belief that they are fundamentally unlovable or unworthy of connection. The negative self-talk then fuels the avoidant behavior, creating a self-fulfilling cycle. The fear of rejection keeps them from getting close, which reinforces their negative beliefs about themselves. Understanding the origins and impacts of negative self-perception is crucial for fostering positive change. By recognizing its roots and its detrimental effects, we can begin to challenge these harmful patterns and cultivate a more compassionate and accepting inner voice.

In order to overcome negative self-perception, you need to identify and challenge all your negative self-talk, as well as your cognitive distortions. If you have no idea where to begin with that, don't worry, I've got you covered!

Overcoming Negative Self-Talk

Negative self-talk can be a persistent foe, but it doesn't have to control the narrative. By developing a toolbox of techniques, you can learn to identify its presence, challenge its validity, and ultimately cultivate a more positive inner voice. Here are some practical tools to empower you on this quest:

- Become aware of negative self-talk: The first step is catching the culprit in action. Pay attention to your inner dialogue throughout the day. When feelings of doubt or insecurity arise, listen closely to the thoughts behind them. Are you using harsh, judgmental language? Are you dwelling on past mistakes or catastrophizing about the future? Identifying these patterns is essential for challenging them.

- Challenge negative self-talk: Don't simply accept these thoughts as truth. Question their validity. Are they based on evidence or simply fear? Would you speak to a friend this way? Often, we're much kinder to others than ourselves.

- Practice positive self-talk: Replace negativity with affirmations. Instead of, "I'll never succeed," counter with, "This may be challenging, but I'm capable of learning and growing." Focus on your strengths and past accomplishments.

- Step outside of yourself: Imagine a trusted friend or mentor encountering your situation. What advice would they offer? How might they reframe the challenge? Seeing things from this external perspective can provide a more balanced view.

- Talk it out: Discussing your struggles with a trusted friend, therapist, or counselor can be incredibly helpful. Verbalizing negative thoughts can often weaken their hold, and you can gain valuable support and guidance in dismantling them.

- Put it on the shelf: Sometimes, immediate action isn't necessary. Acknowledge the negative thought, but instead of engaging with it, visualize placing it on a shelf. You can revisit it later if needed, but for now, allow yourself a mental break.

- Focus on the present moment: Negative self-talk often fixates on the past or worries about the future. Mindfulness practices like meditation or deep breathing can help anchor you in the present moment, where self-doubt has less power.

Overcoming Cognitive Distortions

Cognitive distortions, those sneaky mental traps that distort our perception, can fuel negative self-talk and hinder our emotional well-being. But fear not! Just like negative self-talk, we can equip ourselves with tools to identify and challenge these distortions. Here are some practical techniques to help you become a master detective of your own thoughts.

- Catch yourself in the act: Similar to identifying negative self-talk, the first step is becoming aware of cognitive distortions. When experiencing intense emotions like anxiety or anger, pay attention to your thought patterns. Are you jumping to conclusions, catastrophizing, or personalizing everything? Recognizing these distortions is half the battle.

- Label the distortion: Once you've identified a distorted thought, name the specific type of distortion. Is it all-or-nothing thinking (e.g., "If I don't get this promotion, I'm a complete failure") or filtering out the positive (e.g., "I messed up on that presentation, everything else I did must be worthless")? Labeling the distortion helps you detach from it emotionally and analyze it objectively.

- Challenge the evidence: Now comes the fun part: challenging the distorted thought! Ask yourself questions like, "Is there any evidence to support this thought?" or, "Would I believe this if someone else said it about themself?" Often, when we examine the facts, the distortion crumbles.

- Reality check: Seek a more balanced perspective. Would a trusted friend or objective observer agree with your distorted thought? Sometimes, talking it out with someone can reveal how skewed our thinking might be.

- Reframe the thought: Rewrite the distorted thought into a more realistic and empowering one. For example, instead of, "I'll never be good at public speaking," try, "Public speaking makes me nervous, but I can practice and improve." Reframing allows you to approach challenges with a more positive and solution-oriented mindset.

- Use humor—sparingly: Sometimes, a little humor can go a long way. If you catch yourself catastrophizing about a situation, try injecting a bit of lightheartedness. This can defuse the emotional intensity and help you see the situation from a less distorted lens.

With consistent effort, you'll develop the skills to identify and dismantle these distortions, paving the way for a more positive and resilient mindset.

Replacing Negative Thoughts

Negative thoughts can be persistent, but there are numerous strategies to gradually shift them toward a more positive and realistic perspective. Here's a breakdown of how each method can help.

Start a Journal

Journaling provides a safe space to acknowledge and explore your negative thoughts without judgment. By writing them down, you gain some distance and can begin to analyze them more objectively. This process can help you identify patterns and triggers, paving the way for replacing negativity with more balanced thoughts.

Always Ask Yourself, "What Would I Say to a Friend?"

We tend to be much kinder and more supportive toward our friends than ourselves. By asking yourself how you would comfort a friend experiencing similar negativity, you tap into a wellspring of compassion and gain a more objective perspective. This shift in perspective can help you reframe your own negative thoughts with more positive self-talk.

Say, "Stop"

This simple technique can be surprisingly effective. When you catch yourself dwelling on a negative thought, say, "Stop" or another word that works for you. This brief interruption disrupts the momentum of negativity and creates a space to choose a more positive thought.

Change Negativity to Neutrality

Sometimes, aiming for positivity right away can feel overwhelming. A gentler approach is to first try shifting negativity to neutrality. Instead of, "I'm a failure," try, "This task was challenging." Neutralizing the thought reduces its emotional power and creates a more open mind for introducing a positive alternative later.

Create an SOS File of Positive Praise

This *file* can be physical or digital. Collect quotes, affirmations, or past compliments that remind you of your strengths and accomplishments. When negativity strikes, pull out your SOS file and give yourself a much-needed dose of positivity.

Breathe

Deep breathing activates the relaxation response in your body, counteracting the physical effects of stress and anxiety that often fuel negative thoughts. Taking a few slow, mindful breaths can help you calm down and approach your thoughts with greater clarity, making space for more positive rebuttals.

Talk to Somebody

Sharing your struggles with a trusted friend, therapist, or counselor can be incredibly cathartic. Verbalizing negative thoughts can weaken their hold, and you can gain valuable support and guidance from someone who cares. Hearing a different perspective can also help you identify and challenge cognitive distortions that might be fueling negativity.

Follow a Healthy Lifestyle

Taking care of your physical health goes hand in hand with emotional well-being. Eating nutritious foods, getting enough sleep, and regularly exercising can boost your mood and energy levels, making you more resilient in the face of negativity. A healthy lifestyle provides a foundation for fostering a more positive outlook.

Identify Areas to Change

Sometimes, negativity stems from genuine problems in your life. By identifying areas that need improvement (e.g., setting boundaries or improving communication skills), you can take action to address them. Progress in these areas can naturally replace negativity with a sense of empowerment and accomplishment.

Surround Yourself With Positive People

The people you spend time with significantly influence your thoughts and emotions. Seek out positive individuals who uplift and support you. Their optimism can be contagious and can help you develop a more positive outlook on life.

Practice Self-Compassion

Treat yourself with the same kindness and understanding you would offer a close friend. Recognize that negative thoughts are a normal part of the human experience, and don't beat yourself up for having them. Self-compassion allows you to approach your thoughts with acceptance and opens the door to fostering a more positive inner critic.

Practice Positive Self-Talk Out Loud

Our inner voice is powerful. By consciously choosing positive affirmations and repeating them out loud, you can start to reprogram your subconscious mind. Positive self-talk combats negativity at its source, gradually replacing it with more empowering and realistic beliefs.

Building Positive Self-Identity and Assertiveness

Our sense of self, who we believe ourselves to be, is a fundamental building block for a happy and fulfilling life. A positive self-identity is closely linked to good mental health, impacting everything from our confidence to our relationships. By cultivating a positive self-identity, you will become more confident. When you believe in yourself and your abilities, it allows you to take on challenges and pursue goals. This can lead to a sense of accomplishment and overall satisfaction. On the other hand, a negative self-identity can be detrimental. When we see ourselves in a negative light, it can lead to feelings of inadequacy and low self-worth. This can manifest as anxiety, insecurity, and even depression. Developing a positive self-identity is an ongoing process, but the benefits are undeniable. By nurturing a strong sense of self, we invest in our mental well-being and create the foundation for healthy, fulfilling relationships. So, how do we build a stronger self-identity? Let's have a look!

Exercises to Build Stronger Self-Identity

Your journey to a positive self-identity starts now! Here are some exercises to get you started:

- Build positive relationships: Surrounding yourself with supportive people who uplift and encourage you is crucial. Spend time with those who make you feel good about yourself. This could involve reconnecting with old friends, joining a club, or taking a class to meet new people who share your interests.

- Embrace self-reflection: Take time to reflect on who you are and what matters to you. Journaling is a great tool. Write down your thoughts, feelings, strengths, and weaknesses. Ask yourself questions like: "What are my values?" "What are my goals?" "What makes me happy?"

- The power of affirmations: *Positive affirmations* are "statements that challenge negative self-beliefs." Repeat positive affirmations daily, such as, "I am worthy and capable" or, "I am deserving of love and happiness." Over time, these affirmations can help reprogram your thinking and build self-compassion.

- Practice mindfulness: *Mindfulness* is "the practice of paying attention to the present moment without judgment." Meditation is a form of mindfulness that can help you become more aware of your thoughts and feelings. By observing your thoughts without judgment, you can begin to separate yourself from negative self-talk. There are many guided meditations available online or through apps.

- Seek treatment—if needed: Sometimes, negative self-identity can be rooted in deeper issues. If you're struggling with persistent negative thoughts or low self-esteem, don't hesitate to seek professional help. A therapist can provide guidance and support in developing a healthier self-image.

Overall, becoming more assertive and growing more confident in yourself will enable you to overcome your avoidant attachment style, even if you might not see it now. So, with that being said, let's take a look at a couple of strategies for becoming more assertive.

Becoming More Assertive

Expressing your needs clearly and confidently is a key part of being assertive. Here are some strategies to help you master this skill:

- Value yourself and your rights: The foundation of assertiveness is self-respect. Acknowledge your worth and believe that your needs deserve to be heard. Educate yourself about your rights in different situations—workplace, personal relationships, etc.

- Speak your truth—confidently: Don't be afraid to voice your needs and wants directly. Use "I" statements to avoid accusatory language. For example, instead of saying, "You're always interrupting me," try, "I feel unheard when you interrupt me. Can we wait until I finish speaking?"

- You can't control others, but you can control you: Remember, you can't control how others react to your assertiveness. However, you can control how you express yourself. Focus on your needs and clearly communicate them, but be prepared to accept different perspectives.

- Positivity is power: Frame your requests and needs in a positive light. Instead of complaining, offer solutions. For example, instead of saying, "I can't work this late," try, "I would be happy to complete this by tomorrow morning, but staying late tonight wouldn't work for me."

- Embrace feedback: Being open to both criticism and compliments is a sign of emotional maturity. Use constructive criticism to improve your communication skills, and acknowledge compliments graciously.

- The power of "no": Assertiveness includes the ability to say "no" confidently when something doesn't align with your needs or schedule. Don't feel obligated to justify your reasons for declining a request. A simple "No, thank you" is enough.

- Track your progress: Developing assertiveness takes time and practice. Celebrate your successes, no matter how small. Reflect on situations where you could have been more assertive, and use those experiences to guide your future interactions.

By incorporating these strategies, you can become more assertive in expressing your needs, fostering healthier and more respectful relationships in all areas of your life. Remember, assertiveness is about advocating for yourself while still being respectful of others. It's a win-win!

Perusing Personal Goals

Have a big dream you want to achieve? Maybe it's learning a new language, running a marathon, or starting your own business. Whatever your goal is, the path to success requires a roadmap. Here are some key strategies to help you pursue and achieve your personal goals:

- SMART goals from the start: It all begins with setting SMART goals. Specific, Measurable, Attainable, Relevant, and Time-bound. A vague goal like *get healthier* is less motivating than a SMART goal like *lose 10 lbs in 3 months by exercising 3 times a week for 30 minutes.*

- Pen it down: Writing down your goals makes them more tangible and real. This can be a physical journal or a digital document. The act of physically writing increases your commitment.

- Keep your goals front and center: Place your written goals where you'll see them every day. This could be on your bathroom mirror, refrigerator, or phone wallpaper. Regularly seeing your goals keeps them top of mind and fuels your motivation.

- Break it down, Break it Up: Large goals can feel overwhelming. Break them down into smaller, more manageable steps. This will make the process seem less daunting and help you track your progress.

- Craft a master plan: Develop a clear plan outlining the steps you need to take to achieve your goal. Research resources, identify milestones, and set deadlines for each step.

- Action is key: Don't get stuck in planning mode! Take action and start working toward your goal, even if it's just a small step each day. Consistency is key to progress.

- Maintain perspective: There will be setbacks and challenges along the way. Keep the bigger picture in mind, and don't get discouraged by temporary roadblocks. Celebrate your wins, big and small.

- Find your accountability partner: Having someone to hold you accountable can be a powerful motivator. Share your goals with a friend, family member, or coach who will support and encourage you.

By following these strategies, you can transform your goals from distant aspirations to tangible achievements.

Preserving Individuality While in Relationships

A strong relationship thrives on shared experiences and connection, but it's equally important to nurture your individuality. Here are some strategies to strike that perfect balance:

- Embrace *me time and we time*: Schedule dedicated time for both solo activities and quality time with your partner. Pursue hobbies and interests that bring you joy, even if your partner doesn't share them. This *me time* allows you to recharge and rediscover yourself.

- Communication is key: Openly communicate your need for individuality to your partner. Explain how having separate interests strengthens the relationship by bringing fresh perspectives and experiences to share.

- Celebrate differences: View your individual interests as strengths, not deficits. Your unique passions can add variety and spark to your relationship. Encourage your partner to explore their own hobbies and interests as well.

- Maintain your social circle: Continue nurturing relationships with friends and family outside your romantic partnership. Having a strong support system beyond your partner provides a sense of belonging and fosters personal growth.

- Pursue personal goals: Don't put your personal goals on hold for the relationship. Continue striving for your own achievements and aspirations. Your partner should be your biggest cheerleader, supporting your individual growth.

- Respect boundaries: Healthy boundaries are essential. Communicate your need for space and respect your partner's as well. Don't feel obligated to be together every minute.

- Be open to trying new things: While maintaining individuality, explore new activities together. This can be a fun way to bond and discover shared interests while still fostering personal growth as a couple.

- Remember, you are still *you*: Don't lose sight of who you are as an individual within the relationship. Maintain your unique quirks, opinions, and sense of style. A healthy relationship allows you to grow together while cherishing who you are as separate people.

- Check-in regularly: Talk openly with your partner about how you're both feeling about the balance between togetherness and individuality. Are you both getting enough *me time* and *we time*? Be willing to adjust your approach as needed to ensure a fulfilling relationship for both of you.

By following these tips, you can cultivate a fulfilling relationship where you can thrive as a couple while cherishing your unique identities. Remember, a strong relationship is built on mutual respect, support, and the freedom to be yourself.

Lifestyle Changes

Beyond all the incredible tools and strategies we just discussed, there are a few lifestyle changes that can also help you develop self-esteem and resilience. Remember, without strong self-esteem, you won't be able to manage a healthy relationship. If you want the prize, you have to put in the work and make some sacrifices along the way.

Some sacrifices might include these lifestyle changes. Let's have a look.

Regular Exercise

Feeling overwhelmed and lacking confidence? Consider incorporating regular physical exercise into your routine. It's a practical lifestyle change with powerful benefits for your mental well-being. Exercise strengthens not just your body but also your mind. The sense of accomplishment you gain from physically pushing yourself translates to a boost in self-esteem. Additionally, the release of endorphins during exercise combats stress and negativity, leaving you feeling more resilient and able to bounce back from challenges. Regular physical activity can even improve your decision-making skills and sharpen your focus, making you feel more capable of tackling life's obstacles. So why not give it a try? Even small amounts of exercise can make a big difference in how you see yourself and your ability to handle whatever comes your way.

Healthy Eating

Nourish your body, nourish your self-esteem! Think of healthy eating as a powerful act of self-love. Our bodies are incredible machines, allowing us to experience the world and achieve our goals. When we fuel them with nutritious food, we show them appreciation for their hard work. This simple act of self-care goes a long way in boosting self-esteem. After all, taking care of yourself is a sign of self-worth, and feeling good about the choices you make regarding your health translates into a more confident and resilient you.

Adequate Sleep

Catching those zzz's is more than just about feeling well-rested; it's a key player in building self-esteem and resilience, too! Studies have shown that people who skimp on sleep, getting less than six hours a night, tend to have lower self-esteem compared to those who get a good seven or eight hours. Prioritizing sleep is a simple yet powerful way to feel better about yourself. When you're well-rested, you're naturally more confident, energized to tackle challenges, and better equipped to bounce back from setbacks. So, make sleep a nonnegotiable part of your self-care routine. You'll be amazed at how much better you will feel overall, both inside and out!

For the Partner

When your partner is working on building self-esteem and resilience, your support is crucial. Here are some simple techniques to offer constructive feedback in a way that empowers them:

- Focus on the effort, not the outcome: Did your partner put in a lot of effort on a project even if the result wasn't perfect? Acknowledge their hard work and dedication. "I saw how much time and effort you put into that presentation. It takes a lot of courage to put yourself out there."

- Use "I" statements: "I" statements shift the focus from blame to your own feelings. "I feel worried when you talk down about yourself." This approach is less accusatory and opens the door for a productive conversation.

- Offer specific examples: Instead of a vague "You can do better," offer specific ways your partner can improve. For example, "Your writing is great, but maybe adding a transition sentence here would make the flow smoother."

- Focus on strengths: Before suggesting improvements, highlight your partner's strengths. "You're such a creative problem solver. How can we use that strength to tackle this situation?" This approach builds confidence before addressing weaknesses.

- Ask open-ended questions: Encourage your partner to find their own solutions. "What do you think went well in that meeting?" or "How do you feel we can approach this next time?" This fosters self-reliance and critical thinking.

- Celebrate progress, not perfection: Recognize and celebrate even small improvements. "I noticed you were more assertive in that conversation today. That's awesome!" Positive reinforcement motivates your partner to keep striving.

Mindful Milestone

For the next seven days, commit to incorporating positive affirmations and self-compassion practices into your daily routine. You'll need a journal and a pen, and the rest is up to you!

Daily Activities

Morning Affirmations—5 minutes

1. Start each day by repeating positive affirmations that resonate with you. Here are some examples: "I am worthy of love and happiness." "I am capable of achieving my goals." "I am strong and resilient." You can find more affirmations online or create your own based on your personal needs.

2. Write down your chosen affirmations in your journal and repeat them aloud while looking in the mirror.

Self-Compassion Practice—10 minutes

Choose a self-compassion exercise from the following options, or find one that works for you online:

- **Loving-kindness meditation:** This meditation involves sending well-wishes to yourself and others.
- **Gratitude list:** Write down three to five things you're grateful for each day.
- **The "Inner Critic vs. Inner Champion" dialogue:** Imagine a conversation between your inner critic—negative self-talk—and your inner champion—positive self-talk. Write down their arguments and encourage your inner champion to overpower the negativity.

Evening Reflection—5 minutes

Before bed, reflect on your day in your journal. Note any instances of negative self-talk and challenge them with positive affirmations. Write down any positive experiences you had and how they made you feel. Did you notice any changes in your self-perception throughout the day?

Documenting Your Journey

Throughout the week, track your progress in your journal. Pay attention to any shifts in your self-talk, mood, or confidence levels. Did you find it easier to silence negative self-criticism? Did your overall outlook on life become more positive?

Sharing Is Caring

At the end of the week, reflect on your experience as a whole. Did this challenge impact your self-esteem? Would you recommend this practice to others? Consider sharing your journey and insights with a friend, family member, or online forum.

Remember, self-compassion and positive affirmations are powerful tools for building a stronger, more positive you. This week is just the beginning! By incorporating these practices into your daily routine, you can cultivate lasting change and unlock your full potential. I hope this chapter has inspired you to build self-esteem and resilience, as you now know just how important those two elements are for healthy relationships. In the next chapter, we'll look at how to form and maintain secure relationships, so be sure to stick around; it's going to be a good one.

Chapter 7:
Form and Maintain Secure Relationships

Up until now, we've put in a lot of work and time to understand our own attachment style, especially those of us who struggle with the avoidant attachment style. But we've now reached that point in the journey where we need to look toward the future. What is the point of understanding our attachment style? Where do we go from here? Well, the goal was never to *just* understand your avoidant attachment style. The goal is to transform yourself, going from avoidant to secure attachment. It might sound intimidating, but you're ready! Trust me! If you've put in the work of the previous six chapters, give yourself a pat on the back. All of that work, all of the soul-searching and mindful moments have led you to a place where you can now begin to form and maintain secure relationships.

In this chapter, we'll start by looking at how to begin the transition from avoidant to secure. We'll look at how to nurture healthy and lasting relationships, as well as cultivate an environment that sets your relationships up for success. We can't have a chapter on transforming to secure attachment without addressing the importance of communication, so we'll end this chapter by exploring some of the communication skills you need to embrace in order to grow a secure attachment. So, with all of that being said, let's leave behind the guarded walls and build open doorways for our relationships. As you embrace your vulnerability and navigate potential anxieties, you'll discover the joy and strength that come from truly connecting with others.

From Avoidant to Secure Attachment

The path to secure relationships begins with self-discovery. Recognizing the patterns of avoidant attachment in your own behavior isn't a condemnation; it's the first step on a journey of growth. Imagine your attachment style as a well-worn path: It shows how you currently navigate relationships, but it doesn't have to dictate your final destination. The key to unlocking change lies in understanding that behaviors, not labels, hold the true power. While the term *avoidant attachment* might feel fixed, the reality is that these behaviors are flexible and can be reshaped. The patterns you rely on today are simply habits, and like any habit, they can be unlearned and replaced with new, healthier approaches.

This transformation won't happen overnight. It requires consistent self-awareness, dedication to growth, and a willingness to step outside your comfort zone. It might feel daunting at first, but remember, you're not alone on this journey. There will be moments of uncertainty and setbacks along the way, but with perseverance, you'll develop the tools and confidence to navigate them effectively. As you move beyond avoidance and embrace vulnerability, you'll discover a world of possibilities. You'll unlock the potential for deeper intimacy, forge stronger connections, and experience the joy that comes from truly connecting with others. The rewards for cultivating a secure attachment style are truly life-changing.

So, it's safe to conclude that shifting from avoidance to secure attachment requires not just a behavior change but also a transformation in your mindset and emotional understanding. Here are some key areas to focus on.

Tend to Your Relationship Garden

Think of your relationships as a garden. Secure attachment is the fertile soil that allows connections to thrive. Just like a garden, relationships need consistent care and attention. Invest time and effort in nurturing your bonds with open communication, empathy, and emotional availability.

Don't Make Assumptions, Collect Data

Our brains are wired to make snap judgments, but in relationships, assumptions can be dangerous. When anxieties arise, resist the urge to jump to conclusions. Instead, practice *collecting data*. Communicate openly with your partner or friend, seek clarification, and understand the situation before reacting.

Everyone Is Doing the Best They Can

Approach your interactions with the understanding that everyone, including yourself, is acting from their unique perspective and experiences. This fosters compassion and reduces the tendency to take things personally. When someone upsets you, try to see things from their viewpoint. This doesn't mean excusing bad behavior but allowing for a more understanding and productive response.

Don't Shy Away From Disagreement

Healthy relationships don't require constant agreement. Differences of opinion are inevitable. Secure individuals view disagreements as opportunities for growth and connection. Learn to navigate conflict constructively. Focus on finding common ground, actively listen to the other person's perspective, and be willing to compromise.

Ask Yourself, "What Will It Take to Forgive?"

Holding onto grudges hinders emotional intimacy. When someone hurts you, acknowledge the pain, but also consider what forgiveness might look like for you. Is it an apology? A behavior change? Focusing on forgiveness allows you to move forward and build a stronger relationship.

Nurturing Healthy and Lasting Relationships

As you move from avoidant to secure attachment, you will begin to nurture healthy and lasting relationships. This might be challenging at first, especially if you're not sure what a healthy relationship even looks like. To help you out, let's explore three of the most essential aspects of a healthy and lasting relationship that you'll begin to focus on as you make this life-changing transition.

Openness

This is the cornerstone of trust and intimacy. It's the willingness to share your thoughts, feelings, and vulnerabilities with others (*Embracing Openness,* 2024). Openness involves honest communication, both verbally and nonverbally. It's about expressing your joys and celebrating victories with loved ones, but also being brave enough to share your fears, anxieties, and disappointments. By being open, you create a safe space for genuine connection and allow others to truly know and support you. This vulnerability fosters a sense of emotional security within the relationship, where both partners feel comfortable expressing themselves authentically.

Empathy

Stepping outside your own perspective and trying to understand the world through another person's eyes is crucial for building secure relationships. Empathy allows you to connect with others on a deeper level, fostering compassion and understanding (Reid, 2023b). When your partner is struggling, being able to see things from their viewpoint allows you to offer support that truly resonates. Imagine your partner is feeling hurt by a comment. Instead of reacting defensively, empathy allows you to validate their feelings, perhaps by saying, "I can see why that would be hurtful," and then seeking to understand their perspective. This creates a sense of partnership and strengthens the bond.

Consistent Effort

Relationships, like gardens, require ongoing attention. Don't expect secure attachment to develop overnight. It takes dedicated effort over time. This doesn't mean grand gestures every day but rather a commitment to the small, consistent actions that build trust and connection. Schedule quality time with loved ones, actively listen to their concerns, and celebrate their successes. A simple act of putting away your phone during dinner to focus on conversation, offering a listening ear when they need to vent, or sending a thoughtful message expressing your appreciation can make a big difference. Remember, even small, consistent efforts have a powerful impact on nurturing and maintaining healthy connections. Over time, these actions demonstrate your commitment to the relationship and create a sense of security and stability that allows secure attachment to flourish (Shenoy, 2024).

By embracing these core principles, you'll cultivate a fertile ground for secure attachment to take root. Open communication, emotional understanding, and consistent investment in your relationships will empower you to build strong, lasting connections and experience the joy of true intimacy.

Cultivating a Supportive Relationship Environment

The foundation of secure attachment is a supportive and understanding relationship environment. Here are some practical strategies you can implement to cultivate this kind of space.

Active Listening

This goes beyond simply hearing the words your partner is saying. Active listening involves giving your partner your full attention, making eye contact, and offering verbal and nonverbal cues that show you're engaged. Ask clarifying questions, summarize what you've heard to ensure understanding, and avoid interrupting. This demonstrates your genuine interest in their thoughts and feelings, fostering a sense of security and trust within the relationship.

Space

Everyone needs time and space to process their emotions and navigate challenges on their own. If your partner is feeling overwhelmed or needs some alone time, respect their boundaries. This doesn't mean indifference; it shows respect for their autonomy and allows them to return to the relationship feeling refreshed and ready to connect. Think of emotional intimacy as a dance; sometimes, you need to hold each other close, and sometimes, you need to give each other room to move freely, knowing you'll come back together stronger.

Checking In

Make time for regular conversations that go beyond the mundane. Express interest in their day, thoughts, and feelings. This could be a dedicated daily check-in or simply taking advantage of pockets of time throughout the day to connect. Ask open-ended questions that encourage them to share their experiences. Maybe it's a quick chat over coffee in the morning, a dedicated *catch-up* time after work, or simply taking a few minutes before bed to share highlights from your day. By consistently showing interest in your partner's world, you create a space where they feel comfortable sharing openly and know they have your unwavering support.

Physical Affection

Physical touch is a powerful way to communicate love, affection, and security. A hug, a kiss, holding hands, these gestures don't need to be grand, but they speak volumes. The frequency and type of physical touch will vary depending on the couple, so find what works for you and make it a regular part of your connection. Cuddle on the couch, offer a shoulder rub after a stressful day, or simply hold hands while walking. These small acts of tenderness create a sense of closeness and reinforce the emotional bond.

Own Needs

You can't pour from an empty cup. Taking care of your physical and emotional well-being is essential for building a supportive relationship environment. Schedule time for self-care activities that help you relax and recharge. This might be exercise, spending time in nature, pursuing hobbies, or simply getting enough sleep. Communicate your needs openly to your partner. Maybe you need a quiet night to unwind after a long week, or perhaps you crave some time to pursue a personal interest. By prioritizing your well-being, you ensure you have the emotional reserves to nurture the relationship and be a supportive partner in return.

Don't underestimate the power of shared experiences! As you move forward on this journey of cultivating secure attachment, actively seek out activities that promote closeness and bonding with your partner, friends, or family. Whether it's trying a new recipe together, taking a weekend getaway, or simply enjoying a board game night, these shared moments create lasting memories and strengthen your connection. So, go ahead, explore new hobbies together, laugh over silly games, or engage in meaningful conversations. Embrace the joy of shared experiences and watch your relationships flourish.

Communication Skills and Boundaries

Clear and assertive communication is the lifeblood of healthy relationships. It allows you to express your needs, wants, and feelings honestly and directly while also respecting the thoughts and emotions of your partner. Unlike passive communication, which involves bottling up your feelings, or aggressive communication, which comes across as demanding or hostile, assertiveness finds the middle ground. Being assertive means communicating with others in a direct, honest, and respectful way. It's about expressing yourself clearly and confidently without sugarcoating your message or resorting to forcefulness or aggression. This approach fosters a safe space for open dialogue where both partners feel heard and understood.

In the context of relationships, assertiveness is crucial for establishing and maintaining healthy boundaries. It empowers you to express your needs and expectations directly while also being open to your partner's perspective. For instance, if you feel overwhelmed with household chores, you can assertively communicate this by saying, "I'd appreciate it if we could share the cleaning responsibilities more equally. It would really help me out." This approach is clear, direct, and respectful, fostering a conversation where you can find a solution that works for both of you.

Assertiveness also plays a vital role in maintaining your sense of identity within a relationship. It allows you to express your disagreements and desires without compromising your values. Imagine your partner wants to attend a social event you'd rather skip. Assertiveness allows you to communicate this by saying, "I appreciate you wanting to go, but I'm not really feeling up for it this time. Maybe we can find another activity to do together next weekend?" This approach avoids resentment and allows you to maintain your individuality while still nurturing the relationship.

By mastering assertive communication, you'll equip yourself with the tools to navigate difficult conversations, resolve conflict constructively, and build a strong foundation for secure and lasting connections. Remember, assertiveness isn't about dominance; it's about fostering mutual respect and understanding, which are the cornerstones of any healthy relationship.

Tips for Effective Communication

Mastering assertive communication takes practice, but the rewards are well worth the effort. Here are some practical tips and examples to guide you.

- Process your feelings first: Before diving into a potentially charged conversation, take a moment to collect yourself. Identify your emotions and what you truly want to achieve from the discussion. This will allow you to communicate clearly and avoid letting strong emotions cloud your message.

- Timing is key: Choose a time when you can both have a calm and focused conversation. Avoid initiating difficult discussions when one of you is tired, stressed, or already feeling overwhelmed.

- "I" statements lead the way: Instead of accusatory statements that put your partner on the defensive, start with "I" statements that focus on your feelings. For example, instead of saying, "You never listen to me," try, "I feel frustrated when I feel like I'm not being heard." Owning your own emotions fosters empathy and opens the door for a productive conversation.

- Two-way street: Communication is a two-way street. Practice active listening by giving your partner your full attention, making eye contact, and avoiding interruptions. Acknowledge their perspective by reflecting back on what you've heard and seeking clarification if needed.

- Seek resolution, not just understanding: While understanding is important, the ultimate goal of communication is often to find a solution that works for both of you. Frame the conversation around compromise and be open to finding common ground. Perhaps you can brainstorm solutions together or agree to table the discussion and revisit it later with a fresh perspective.

- Boundaries—a must-have: Healthy relationships require clear boundaries. Assertive communication empowers you to set these boundaries directly and respectfully. For instance, you can say, "I need some personal time in the evenings to unwind. Would you mind if we planned social activities for the weekends?"

- Leave notes: A quick note expressing appreciation or a reminder can go a long way. This could be a sweet message left on the bathroom mirror, a grocery list with a playful note, or a simple *thinking of you* text. These small gestures demonstrate you care and keep communication flowing throughout the day.

- Regular check-ins: Schedule regular check-ins with your partner, even if it's just a few minutes at the end of the day. These dedicated moments allow you to connect, share updates, and address any small issues before they escalate.

By incorporating these tips into your daily interactions, you'll cultivate a space where both you and your partner feel heard, respected, and understood. This paves the way for stronger bonds, deeper intimacy, and the secure, fulfilling relationships you deserve.

For the Partner

It's wonderful that your partner is actively working toward a secure attachment style! This journey takes time and dedication, but your support can make a world of difference. Here are some tips for nurturing continuous growth together:

- Be patient and understanding: Change doesn't happen overnight. There will be setbacks and moments where your partner falls back into old avoidance patterns. Be patient and understanding. Remind them of their progress and offer support without judgment.

- Manage your expectations: While communication and effort are crucial, avoid pressuring your partner to disclose more than they're comfortable with. Respect their boundaries and allow them to open up at their own pace.

- Remember, you are a team: Approach this journey as a team effort. Support your partner's growth while also prioritizing your own well-being. Communicate openly about your needs and maintain healthy boundaries.

- Celebrate your growth together: As your partner progresses toward a secure attachment style, your relationship will naturally evolve. Celebrate these milestones together! Enjoy the deeper intimacy, stronger connection, and increased emotional security that comes with secure attachment.

Mindful Milestone

Now that you're equipped with the knowledge and tools for assertive communication, it's time to put them into action! Here's your opportunity to initiate or participate in a difficult conversation with a loved one using your newfound communication skills.

Choose Your Conversation

Reflect on your relationships. Is there an ongoing issue with a partner, friend, or family member that's been causing tension? Perhaps you haven't been feeling heard, or there's a lack of trust that needs to be addressed. Choose a situation that feels manageable but also meaningful for growth.

Planning the Conversation

- **Identify your goal:** What do you hope to achieve from this conversation? Is it improved understanding, a change in behavior, or simply a clearer picture of the situation? Having a clear goal will keep the conversation focused and productive.

- **Process your emotions:** Before initiating the conversation, take some time to process your own feelings. Acknowledge your anxieties, frustrations, or hurt, but also identify your underlying desires for the relationship.

Initiating the Conversation

- **Timing is key:** Choose a calm and private moment when you can both have a focused discussion. Avoid bringing up sensitive topics when your loved one is stressed or preoccupied.

- **Start with "I" statements:** Begin by expressing your feelings using "I" statements. For example, "I've been feeling a little disconnected lately, and I'd like to talk about it." This approach sets a non-accusatory tone and opens the door for a heartfelt conversation.

Active Listening and Empathy

- **Listen attentively:** Give your loved one your full attention, make eye contact, and avoid interrupting. Listen without judgment, focusing on understanding their perspective.

- **Acknowledge their feelings:** Validate their emotions by reflecting back on what you've heard and seeking clarification. For instance, "It sounds like you feel unheard when I bring up this topic. Is that right?"

Finding Common Ground

- **Focus on solutions:** Once you've both shared your perspectives, shift the focus toward finding a solution. Brainstorm options together and be open to compromise.
- **Set clear boundaries—if applicable:** If boundaries are a concern, use assertive communication to express your needs clearly and respectfully.

Reflecting on the Experience

Take some time to reflect on the conversation. How did it go? Were you able to communicate effectively? Did you encounter any unexpected challenges? Most importantly, did you experience any emotional breakthroughs or a shift in the dynamic of your relationship?

Remember, communication is a journey, not a destination. There may be bumps along the road, but with consistent effort and a commitment to assertive communication, you'll build stronger, more secure relationships with the people who matter most.

Now that you've started the transformation, you are well on your way to overcoming avoidant attachment style and embracing a new, healthier way of building and maintaining relationships. In the next chapter, we'll embark on the final step of this journey, which is all about overcoming obstacles and embracing lifelong change.

Chapter 8:
Overcome Obstacles and Embrace Change

Can you believe we're already at the final chapter of our journey together? But before you pack up your bags and head for the door, stick around because this chapter is not to be missed. In fact, in many ways, this chapter is essential for understanding the future and being prepared for what is still to come on this journey of transformation from avoidant attachment to secure attachment. Like any road we take in life, we are bound to run into some obstacles, some more intense than others. But regardless, if we're not prepared for these obstacles, it can cause our momentum and progress to come to a stop. But can we prevent these obstacles?

Yes and no. No, we can't prevent the obstacles from threatening our progress, but yes, we can prevent them from causing us to fail or give up. With the right mindset, tools, and motivation, we can be prepared for the obstacles and embrace change with a smile. In this chapter, we'll address four main things that we need in order to make a success of our journey:

- self-compassion
- overcoming doubt and fear
- time management
- patience and perseverance

One by one, we'll look at why these things are essential as we're facing the future, along with how to embrace change and cultivate it in our lives. By the end of this chapter, I hope that you'll feel empowered and motivated to continue strong even as we come to the end of this book. So, are you ready to take these final steps? Let's get right to it!

Self-Compassion

Life throws us curveballs, and navigating them within a relationship can be especially challenging. When setbacks and disagreements arise, self-compassion becomes a powerful tool for fostering resilience and strengthening your bond. Traditionally, we often respond to difficulties with harsh self-criticism, which can be incredibly damaging. Imagine facing a communication breakdown with your partner and then beating yourself up about it. This negativity can spiral, leading to feelings of despair and hindering your ability to move forward productively. This is where self-compassion steps in. It's about treating yourself with the same kindness and understanding you'd offer a close friend in a similar situation. Self-compassion isn't about letting yourself off the hook for bad behavior. It's about acknowledging your shortcomings with kindness and using them as stepping stones for improvement. This allows you to approach your partner with empathy and understanding, fostering a more collaborative and supportive dynamic. Let's look at some strategies for increased self-compassion.

Strategies for Self-Compassion

Now that we know that self-compassion strengthens relationships, we need to explore how to actually practice it. Here are some powerful strategies you can incorporate into your daily life:

Write a Self-Compassion Letter

Imagine your best friend is going through a similar situation. What words of encouragement and understanding would you offer them? Now, write a letter to yourself from that perspective. Pour your heart out, acknowledge the challenges you're facing, and offer yourself kindness and support. Reread this letter when self-doubt creeps in—it's a tangible reminder of your inherent worth.

Take a Self-Compassion Break

When you're feeling overwhelmed or down on yourself, pause and take a self-compassion break. Find a quiet space, close your eyes, and take a few deep breaths. Imagine placing your hands gently over your heart as a gesture of comfort. Silently acknowledge that you're struggling and offer yourself kind words like, "This is a tough time, but I'm strong enough to handle it."

Listen to Self-Compassion Meditation

Guided meditations can be a powerful tool for cultivating self-compassion. Search online for guided meditations specifically focused on self-compassion. These meditations often use gentle prompts and imagery to help you connect with your inner self and cultivate feelings of kindness and understanding.

Keep a Self-Compassion Journal

Journaling is a powerful tool for self-reflection and growth. Dedicate a section of your journal to self-compassion. Write down situations where you struggled or felt down on yourself. Then, challenge those negative thoughts and reframe them with a more compassionate perspective. Over time, this practice can help you develop a more positive inner voice.

Addressing Doubt, Fear, and Past Failures

Transforming from an avoidant attachment style to a secure one is a journey of self-discovery and emotional growth. However, some internal roadblocks can slow progress.

Self-Doubt

- **Challenge:** Self-doubt whispers insecurities, making you question your ability to form healthy, secure relationships. "Can I really trust someone not to hurt me?" This hesitation can prevent you from opening up emotionally and fostering deeper connections.

- **Impact:** Self-doubt can lead to emotional distance and missed opportunities for intimacy. It can also make you overly critical of yourself and your partner's actions, creating unnecessary tension in the relationship.

Fear

- **Challenge:** Fear, often rooted in past experiences, can manifest in various ways. Fear of intimacy might make you build walls to avoid emotional vulnerability. Fear of rejection might prevent you from putting yourself out there and potentially getting hurt.

- **Impact:** Fear can hinder your ability to be present and engaged in a relationship. It can also lead to self-sabotaging behaviors that push potential partners away.

Memories of Past Failures

- **Challenge:** Negative experiences in past relationships can leave emotional scars. Recalling these experiences can trigger anxiety and make you hesitant to trust again.
- **Impact:** Memories of past failures can create a negative bias, making you view new relationships with suspicion. You might project past hurts onto new partners, hindering the development of trust and intimacy.

However, even when faced with these obstacles, you can still be successful in your transformation. It's easy to get discouraged by setbacks, but what if we viewed them as opportunities for growth? By shifting our perspective, we can transform stumbles into stepping stones on the path to stronger, more secure connections. Here's a three-step approach to turn setbacks into learning experiences that benefit your relationships.

From Setback to Growth

Step 1: Acceptance—Acknowledge the Bump in the Road

The first step is acknowledging the situation. Trying to ignore or downplay the issue will only prolong the discomfort. Have an honest conversation with yourself and your partner—if applicable—about what went wrong. Avoid dwelling on blame; instead, focus on what you can learn from the experience.

Step 2: Learning—Unearthing the Gems of Wisdom

Setbacks, while frustrating, often hold valuable lessons. Take time to reflect on what happened. Ask yourself questions like:

- What could I have done differently?

- What could my partner have done differently?—if applicable.

- What are my underlying emotional needs that weren't being met?

By reflecting on these questions, you gain valuable insights into yourself and your relationship dynamics. This knowledge equips you to navigate similar situations more effectively in the future.

Step 3: Goal Setting—Paving the Path for Growth

Once you've learned from the experience, it's time to move forward. Set clear goals for yourself and your relationship—if applicable—based on the insights you gained. These goals could be related to communication, emotional expression, or simply spending more quality time together.

So, the next time you experience a setback in your relationship, remember that it's not the end of the road. It's a chance to learn, grow, and build a stronger connection. Embrace the challenge, and watch your relationships blossom!

Time Management and Motivation

As you navigate the challenges of transforming from an avoidant to a secure attachment style, time management and motivation become crucial allies. Self-compassion practices and goal setting take time and dedication. Hence, scheduling dedicated time for self-reflection and relationship-building fosters progress. Besides, motivation wanes at times, but remember, setbacks are opportunities to learn. By prioritizing self-care and celebrating small victories, you'll stay motivated on your journey toward secure and fulfilling connections.

Here's how you can develop better time management and remain motivated throughout your journey.

Developing Time Management

Transforming your attachment style takes dedication, but feeling overwhelmed by time constraints can hinder progress. Here are some time management tips to empower your self-improvement path:

- Make a plan: Don't wing it! Schedule dedicated time for self-reflection activities like journaling or meditation. Block out time in your calendar for nurturing your relationships, whether it's a date night or a call with a friend.

- Prioritize, don't just list: A to-do list can feel overwhelming. Instead, create a priority list that reflects your self-improvement goals. Focus on the most impactful activities first.

- Chunk it down: Large, looming tasks can paralyze you. Break down your self-improvement goals into smaller, manageable steps. This makes them less daunting and easier to fit into your schedule.

- Decision fatigue is real: Limit the number of daily decisions you make. Plan outfits and meals in advance to free up mental space for self-improvement activities.

- Delegate and say no: Can't do it all? Delegate tasks when possible, or learn to politely decline requests that don't align with your priorities.

- Deadlines keep you accountable: Set realistic deadlines for completing self-improvement tasks. Having a timeframe creates a sense of urgency and helps you stay on track.

- Mind your mind: We all get sidetracked. When you notice your focus drifting, gently redirect your attention back to your self-improvement activity.

- Minimize distractions: Silence notifications, put your phone away, and find a quiet space to minimize distractions during self-reflection or relationship-building activities.

- Manage stress wisely: Feeling overwhelmed? Schedule stress-relieving activities like exercise or spending time in nature. A clear mind is better equipped to handle self-improvement challenges.

- Multitasking myth: Focus on one task at a time. Multitasking is a myth that actually reduces productivity. Give your self-improvement activities your full attention for maximum benefit.

- The power of 20 minutes: Use the *20-minute rule*. Commit to working on a self-improvement task for just 20 minutes. Often, you'll find yourself continuing past the initial timeframe.

- Schedule breaks: Don't burn out! Schedule breaks throughout your day to recharge. Taking time off allows you to return to your self-improvement journey with renewed energy and focus.

- Find your system: Experiment and develop a time management system that works for you. Consistency is key!

Sticking to a system helps you integrate self-improvement activities seamlessly into your daily routine.

By implementing these time management tips, you'll create the space and focus needed to nurture your well-being and build secure, fulfilling relationships.

Maintaining Motivation

Transforming your attachment style and building secure relationships is an ongoing process. Motivation inevitably wanes at times, but there are strategies to keep the fire burning bright.

- Calendar your goals: Don't just dream it, schedule it! Block out dedicated time in your calendar for self-improvement activities. Treating these entries like important appointments increases commitment.

- Habits make change stick: Turn self-improvement practices into daily habits. Schedule meditation right after waking up, or dedicate 10 minutes before bed to journaling. The repetition reinforces the behavior and makes it a natural part of your routine.

- Small wins, big impact: Set small, achievable goals to build momentum. Celebrating small victories keeps you motivated and reinforces positive behavior. Gradually increase the difficulty of your goals as your confidence grows.

- Track your journey: Journaling your progress is a powerful tool. Track your successes, challenges, and learnings. Seeing your progress visually is a great motivator.

- Celebrate every milestone: Don't wait for the finish line to celebrate! Acknowledge and reward yourself for completing even small tasks or achieving mini-goals. This positive reinforcement keeps you moving forward.

- Embrace the power of peers: Surround yourself with positive people who are also on a self-improvement journey. Share your goals and support each other through challenges.

- Gratitude is a motivator: Practice daily gratitude, including expressing appreciation for yourself and your efforts. Recognizing your progress fosters a positive mindset and fuels motivation.

- Mood matters: Feeling down? Engage in mood-lifting activities like exercise, spending time in nature, or listening to uplifting music. A positive mood makes self-improvement efforts feel less daunting.

- Change your scenery: Sometimes, a change of scenery can spark motivation. Find a quiet space dedicated to self-reflection activities, or try a new meditation app.

- Remember your why: When motivation dips, revisit your *why*. Remind yourself of the deeper purpose behind your self-improvement journey. Reconnecting with your core motivation reignites your passion and propels you forward.

There will be setbacks and moments of doubt, but by implementing these strategies, you'll build resilience, maintain motivation, and stay on track toward building secure and fulfilling relationships.

The Importance of Patience and Perseverance

We all crave instant results, but the truth is that transforming your attachment style and building secure relationships is a marathon, not a sprint. Patience becomes your most valuable asset on this journey.

Patience

As the saying goes, *Rome wasn't built in a day.* Unlearning old attachment patterns and developing new, secure ones requires consistent effort over time. Don't get discouraged if progress feels slow. Celebrate the small victories, and trust that with dedication, you'll reach your goals. Without patience, you might get frustrated with the perceived lack of progress and abandon your self-improvement efforts altogether. Patience allows you to stay committed for the long haul, investing the time and energy necessary to see lasting change. Patience may be the most important attribute you need to possess to make meaningful changes in your life because change is hard and slow. Without patience, you won't devote the time and energy necessary to allow those changes to emerge (Taylor, 2023).

By embracing patience, you cultivate a growth mindset. You understand that setbacks are inevitable, but they don't define you. Instead, they become valuable learning experiences that propel you forward on your journey toward secure and fulfilling relationships. But remember, patience is a muscle. The more you cultivate patience in your self-improvement journey, the easier it becomes to apply it to other areas of your life. So, be kind to yourself, celebrate your progress, and trust that with time and dedication, you'll blossom into the secure and connected person you desire to be.

Perseverance

Perseverance is the unwavering commitment to keep moving forward, even when the road gets tough. The journey toward secure relationships isn't always smooth sailing. You'll encounter setbacks, misunderstandings, and moments of doubt. But perseverance ensures you don't give up at the first hurdle. It fuels your determination to learn from challenges, navigate obstacles, and keep moving forward on your path to growth. Perseverance helps you make progress even when things get tough, which is important for future success. When you work toward your goals and dreams, there will be obstacles and setbacks. But if you persevere, you'll make progress and learn a skill that will pay off in the long run (Jenkins, 2022).

By embracing perseverance, you cultivate a growth mindset. You understand that setbacks are inevitable learning experiences, not roadblocks. They become stepping stones on your path toward secure and fulfilling connections.

For the Partner

It's important that you and your partner work together to remain resilient. Life is filled with ups and downs, and part of being a healthy couple means being able to withstand hardships and endure difficult times. Here are some strategies for staying resilient as a couple:

- **Focus on problem-solving, not blame games:** When disagreements surface, approach them collaboratively. Work together to identify the root cause of the issue and brainstorm solutions that address both your needs. This strengthens your ability to navigate challenges as a team.

- **Schedule quality time, but prioritize quality over quantity:** Set aside dedicated time for activities you both enjoy, unplug from distractions, and truly connect. Even small gestures like a daily walk or a shared evening ritual can make a big difference.

- **Express appreciation regularly:** Let your partner know how much you value them, both through words of affirmation and acts of service. Simple gestures like making coffee in the morning or complimenting their efforts can go a long way in strengthening the bond.

- **Maintain healthy individuality:** While nurturing your connection, it's important to maintain your own interests and hobbies. Having fulfilling lives outside the relationship prevents codependency and fosters personal growth, which ultimately benefits the partnership.

- **Cultivate strong friendships and healthy family boundaries:** Having a supportive network of friends and family provides a sense of belonging and reduces stress in the relationship. However, it's also crucial to establish healthy boundaries with external influences to prioritize your time together as a couple.

By prioritizing communication, nurturing connection, and fostering a supportive environment, you and your partner can weather life's storms and emerge even stronger.

Mindful Moment

Strong relationships are essential for our well-being. Let's dive into creating a personal goal to improve how you connect with others!

Define Your Goal

- Reflect on your current relationships. Are there areas you'd like to strengthen, like becoming more open with friends or fostering deeper connections with family?

- Maybe you crave a new social circle and want to focus on building friendships.

- Is there a specific attachment style you'd like to work on, like becoming less anxious or more trusting in relationships?

Break It Down: Steps to Success

Once you have a clear goal, map out the steps to achieve it:

- **Communication skills:** Consider taking a communication course or reading self-help books on active listening and assertive communication.

- **Social expansion:** Research clubs or groups related to your hobbies or volunteer in your community to meet new people with similar interests.

- **Vulnerability practice:** Begin by sharing small things with trusted friends and gradually open up about more personal aspects of your life.

Anticipate Obstacles

- **Time commitment:** Building relationships takes time and effort. Be realistic about what you can manage alongside other commitments.

- **Rejection:** Putting yourself out there can lead to some rejection. Don't let this discourage you—persistence is key.

- **Fear of vulnerability:** Opening up can feel scary. Remind yourself that true connection thrives on authenticity.

Commit to Your Journey

- **Set a timeline:** Assign a timeframe for your goal. Maybe it's developing better communication skills in your relationship over the next three months or expanding your social circle by joining a club within the next month.

- **Track your progress:** Journal about your experiences, successes, and challenges. This can help you stay motivated and measure progress.

- **Celebrate milestones:** Acknowledge your achievements, no matter how small. This reinforces positive behavior and keeps you on track.

As we reach the end of our journey together, it's important that we recap everything we've learned together in order to ensure success for the future. So, before we say our final goodbyes, let's wrap our minds around all the essential information we've learned on this journey. All of that and more are up next in the conclusion.

Conclusion

Have you ever wondered what Gomez Adams from *The Adams Family*, Pam from *The Office*, and Daphne Bridgerton from *Bridgerton* have in common? Well, you probably guessed it! They have a secure attachment style. Unlike our beloved characters in the introduction, these fictional characters are secure in themselves, as well as in their relationships. They don't push their partners away but stand by them when things get hard. They welcome intimacy and vulnerability and show their love openly. They don't let fear of rejection hold them back. Instead, they face their fears and constantly challenge themselves to be loyal and loving and enjoy their relationships to the fullest. They trust their partners and openly communicate when something is bothering them without being on the attack. It sounds pretty nice, doesn't it?

Well, that's what you can have as well! You might have started this journey as someone with an avoidant attachment style, but you now have all the tools you need to transform into the loving partner you've always wanted to be and have successful relationships. What a relief to know that your attachment style isn't a life sentence and that you can actually change it when you put in the work. The fact that you're here, at the end of our journey, means that you're already putting in the work. But it doesn't end now. In fact, this is only the beginning! My time as your guide might be over, but your journey is still going strong! So, if you don't feel like you've changed yet, take a breather and know that it's okay. Change doesn't happen overnight. As long as you continue to work toward the goal, eventually, you will get there with the help of all the tools you've acquired on this journey. Speaking of, let's recap everything we've learned on this expedition together:

1. We started by learning the basics of attachment styles and understanding the different styles a little bit better. This gave us the foundation to know which style to work toward in the end.

2. Then, we looked at avoidant attachment and the roots it can have in our lives. Understanding what it is rooted in helped us on the next steps.

3. After that, we explored what a daily life with avoidant attachment might look like, which enabled us to identify our own behaviors that are linked to our attachment styles.

4. In Chapter 4, we explored the use of the A.R.C. method to overcome our avoidant attachment behavior. We went through all 3 steps and were able to really dig deep into our attachment style.

5. Next, we discovered the importance of self-esteem and resilience when it comes to overcoming your attachment style. This chapter was filled with practical steps and tips for the future.

6. After that, we explored how to form and maintain healthy and secure relationships. We learned what healthy relationships look like and what we can do to achieve them.

7. Finally, we ended the journey by exploring how to overcome the obstacles in our way as we embrace the new change, allowing us to remain motivated and on track.

So, my friend, you have everything you need to make a success of this experience. I know it might seem difficult or perhaps even impossible at this moment, but you can do this! If you have a partner, rely on them. Invite them on the journey with you and ask them for support when it feels too heavy to do on your own. Remember, vulnerability isn't a sign of weakness. It takes strength and courage to admit that you need to change. You've got this!

If you enjoyed this book and found it helpful, please consider leaving a review so that other avoidant attachment persons can find their way to this journey as well. Whatever you do, remember that you have the power to trust others, overcome past failures, build strong relationships, cultivate resilience, and embrace a positive mindset. I can't wait to hear your success stories!

References

Attachment and child development. (2023, August 10). NSPCC Learning. https://learning.nspcc.org.uk/child-health-development/attachment-early-years/#:~:text=Benefits%20of%20secure%20attachment&text=Children%20with%20secure%20attachments%20are

Avoidant attachment style - learn the causes and symptoms. (2020, July 2). Attachment Project. https://www.attachmentproject.com/blog/avoidant-attachment-style/

Cafasso, J. (2019, November 14). *Anxious attachment: Signs in children and adults, causes, and more*. Healthline. https://www.healthline.com/health/mental-health/anxious-attachment#:~:text=What%20Is%20Anxious%20Attachment%3F&text=You%20can%20develop%20an%20anxious

Cassidy, J., Jones, J. D., & Shaver, P. R. (2013). Contributions of attachment theory and research: A framework for future research, translation, and policy. *Development and Psychopathology*, *25*(4pt2), 1415–1434. https://doi.org/10.1017/s0954579413000692

Cherry, K. (2023a, May 19). *What is repetition compulsion?* Verywell Mind. https://www.verywellmind.com/what-is-repetition-compulsion-7253403

Cherry, K. (2023b, September 12). *How John Bowlby influenced child psychology*. Verywell Mind. https://www.verywellmind.com/john-bowlby-biography-1907-1990-2795514#:~:text=explore%20the%20world.-

Claridge, S., & Barry, S. (n.d.). *Resilience for learning: Mental well-being and attachment*. bristol.gov.uk.

https://www.bristol.gov.uk/files/documents/3756-attachment-disorder/file#:~:text=Secure%20Attachment%3A%20Across%20cultures%2055

Diamond, G., Diamond, G. M., & Levy, S. (2021). Attachment-based family therapy: Theory, clinical model, outcomes, and process research. *Journal of Affective Disorders*, *294*, 286–295. https://doi.org/10.1016/j.jad.2021.07.005

Drescher, A. (2024, January 23). *Disorganized attachment style*. Simply Psychology. https://www.simplypsychology.org/disorganized-attachment.html#:~:text=The%20Development%20of%20Disorganized%20Attachment%20Style&text=However%2C%20when%20a%20caregiver%20is

Eatough, E. (2022, May 18). *What is self-motivation? Push yourself to meet your goals*. Better Up. https://www.betterup.com/blog/what-is-self-motivation

Embracing openness: A guide to honest disclosure. (2024, February 23). Faster Capital. https://fastercapital.com/content/Embracing-Openness--A-Guide-to-Honest-Disclosure.html#:~:text=Embracing%20openness%20in%20relationships%20is

Esposito, L. (2016, March 22). *Why do we repeat the past in our relationships?* Psychology Today. https://www.psychologytoday.com/za/blog/anxiety-zen/201603/why-do-we-repeat-the-past-in-our-relationships

Fritscher, L. (2019). *Overcoming a fear of vulnerability and love your imperfections*. Verywell Mind. https://www.verywellmind.com/fear-of-vulnerability-2671820

How attachment styles impact relationships: Healing relational trauma. (2023, August 29). Bay Area CBT Center. https://bayareacbtcenter.com/attachment-styles-relationships-relational-trauma/#:~:text=An%20anxious%20ambivalent%20attachment%20typically

Jenkins, P. (2022, April 26). *Why is perseverance important (explained).* Brilliantio. https://brilliantio.com/why-is-perseverance-important/

Jones, H. (2023, April 27). *What is anxious preoccupied attachment?* Verywell Health. https://www.verywellhealth.com/anxious-attachment-5204408#:~:text=Anxious%20preoccupied%20attachment%E2%80%94also%20known

Lafair, S. (2024, January 30). *The multifaceted nature of intelligence "we are more than a number!"* LinkedIn. https://www.linkedin.com/pulse/multifaceted-nature-intelligence-we-more-than-number-sylvia-lafair-qalvf/

Lahousen, T., Unterrainer, H. F., & Kapfhammer, H.-P. (2019). Psychobiology of attachment and trauma—some general remarks from a clinical perspective. *Frontiers in Psychiatry, 10*(914). https://doi.org/10.3389/fpsyt.2019.00914

Landry, L. (2019). *Why emotional intelligence is important in leadership.* Harvard Business School Online. https://online.hbs.edu/blog/post/emotional-intelligence-in-leadership

Li, P. (2022, August 16). *Avoidant attachment: 10 ways to heal, causes & effects.* Parenting for Brain. https://www.parentingforbrain.com/avoidant-attachment/#:~:text=As%20a%20result%2C%20avoidant%20children

Light, R. (2023, August 22). *Fearful avoidant: The dance of intimacy & fear.* LinkedIn. https://www.linkedin.com/pulse/fearful-avoidant-dance-intimacy-fear-light-pmp-sdlc-agile-safe/

Main, P. (2022, October 24). *Social learning theory - Bandura.* Structural Learning. https://www.structural-learning.com/post/social-learning-theory-bandura

Main, P. (2023, June 30). *Bowlby's attachment theory.* Structural Learning. https://www.structural-learning.com/post/bowlbys-attachment-theory#:~:text=John%20Bowlby%2C%20a%20renowned%20British

Movahed Abtahi, M., & Kerns, K. A. (2017). Attachment and emotion regulation in middle childhood: Changes in affect and vagal tone during a social stress task. *Attachment & Human Development, 19*(3), 221–242. https://doi.org/10.1080/14616734.2017.1291696

Pal, A. (2023, August 23). *Attachment theory: Unraveling the intricate threads that weave our emotional bonds.* LinkedIn. https://www.linkedin.com/pulse/attachment-theory-unraveling-intricate-threads-weave-our-anupama-pal/

Perera, K. (2020, September 13). *What is low self esteem?* More Self Esteem. https://more-selfesteem.com/more-self-esteem/building-self-esteem/what-is-self-esteem/

Pittman, D. (2020, November 14). *What is secure attachment and how does it develop?* Talkspace. https://www.talkspace.com/blog/parenting-secure-attachment-what-is/#:~:text=Into%20adulthood%2C%20secure%20attachment%20translates

Rafferty, B. (2019). *Repetition compulsion and choice of love object*. [Thesis, Dublin Business School]. esource.dbs.ie. https://esource.dbs.ie/server/api/core/bitstreams/5e15bde6-74df-4e39-86f0-6035ef3fe87a/content

Rees, C. (2007). Childhood attachment. *The British Journal of General Practice, 57*(544), 920–922. https://doi.org/10.3399/096016407782317955

Regan, S. (2023, May 24). *Think someone has an avoidant attachment style? Here's how to tell*. Mindbodygreen. https://www.mindbodygreen.com/articles/avoidant-attachment

Reid, S. (2023a, March 22). *Empathy*. Help Guide. https://www.helpguide.org/articles/relationships-communication/empathy.htm

Reid, S. (2023b, October 11). *Empathy: How to feel and respond to the emotions of others*. Help Guide. https://www.helpguide.org/articles/relationships-communication/empathy.htm#:~:text=Empathy%20allows%20you%20to%20deepen

Reisz, S., Duschinsky, R., & Siegel, D. J. (2017). Disorganized attachment and defense: Exploring john bowlby's unpublished reflections. *Attachment & Human Development, 20*(2), 107–134. https://doi.org/10.1080/14616734.2017.1380055

Robinson, L., Segal, J., & Jaffe, J. (2024, February 19). *Attachment styles and how they affect adult relationships*. Help Guide. https://www.helpguide.org/articles/relationships-communication/attachment-and-adult-relationships.htm#:~:text=fears%20of%20intimacy.-

Secure attachment style: A definition. (2021, September 9). Perth Counselling and Psychotherapy. https://perthcounsellingandpsychotherapy.com.au/secure-attachment-style-a-definition/#:~:text=People%20with%20secure%20attachment%20are

Segal, J., Smith, M., Robinson, L., & Shubin, J. (2024, February 5). *Improving emotional intelligence (EQ)*. Help Guide. https://www.helpguide.org/articles/mental-health/emotional-intelligence-eq.htm#:~:text=Your%20relationships.

Shenoy, S. (2024, March 15). *The compound effect: How small habits can create big changes in your life*. The Dream Catcher. https://thedreamcatch.com/the-compound-effect-how-small-habits-can-create-big-changes-in-your-life/#:~:text=power%20of%20compounding.-

Smith Haghighi, A. (2020, November 12). *Avoidant attachment: Symptoms, signs, causes, and more*. Medical News Today. https://www.medicalnewstoday.com/articles/avoidant-attachment#:~:text=Children%20with%20avoidant%20attachment%20may%20also%20disconnect%20from%20their%20own

Taylor, J. (2023, June 12). *The power of patience for positive life change*. Psychology Today. https://www.psychologytoday.com/us/blog/the-power-of-prime/202306/the-power-of-patience-for-positive-life-change

Understanding the impact of trauma. (2014). National Library of Medicine; Substance Abuse and Mental Health Services Administration (US). https://www.ncbi.nlm.nih.gov/books/NBK207191/#:~:text=As%20a%20clear%20example%2C%20early

www.ingramcontent.com/pod-product-compliance
Ingram Content Group UK Ltd.
Pitfield, Milton Keynes, MK11 3LW, UK
UKHW020835090625
6297UKWH00047B/1347